EXCLUDED MEN

Men who are missing from education and training

EXCLUDED MEN

Men who are missing
from education and training

Veronica McGivney

NIACE
THE NATIONAL ORGANISATION
FOR ADULT LEARNING

Published by the National Institute of
Adult Continuing Education (England and Wales)

21 De Montfort Street
Leicester LE1 7GE
Company registration no. 2603322
Charity registration no. 1002775

First published 1999

NIACE
THE NATIONAL ORGANISATION
FOR ADULT LEARNING

NIACE, the national organisation for adult learning,
has a broad remit to promote lifelong learning
opportunities for adults. NIACE works to develop
increased participation in education and training,
particularly for those who do not have easy access
because of barriers of class, gender, age, race,
language and culture, learning difficulties and
disabilities, or insufficient financial resources.

NIACE's website on the Internet is http://www.niace.org.uk

Cataloguing in Publication Data
A CIP record of this title is available from the British Library

Designed and typeset by Boldface
Printed in Great Britain by Alden Press

ISBN: 1 86202 039 0

Contents

List of tables

Acknowledgements

I am very grateful to my colleagues Sue Cara, Alan Clarke, Stephen McNair, Bryan Merton, Jim Soulsby and Alastair Thomson for suggestions and contacts, and to Tracey Morris and Helen Jones for their help with diagrams and references.

For information on their work I am indebted to:

Katie Clarricoates, New Horizons and Community Centre Belvoir High school, Bottesford

Moria Coleman, Workers' Educational Association, Trailblazer project director

Mary Crowley, Waltham Forest Adult Education Service

Colin Neville, courses organiser, Personal and Professional Development Programme, University of Bradford

Michael Pocock, and Dave Jordan, Farnborough College of Technology

Introduction

Central to the work of the National Institute of Adult Continuing Education (NIACE) is a concern with extending learning opportunities to all segments of the population, especially those disadvantaged by poverty, race, age, disability or place of residence. As part of this remit, NIACE has recognised the importance of creating appropriate educational pathways for women and this rightly remains an important objective for many adult educators. In recent years, however, some providers have become worried at the absence of men, particularly working class men, from post-compulsory education and training. They have found that whenever new access initiatives and learning opportunities are created, it is invariably women who take most advantage of them. This desk study has been conducted in response to this concern. It is based on the findings of existing research, surveys of male participants and non-participants and the views and observations of practitioners. The principal aims were to investigate the reasons for male non-participation, and to identify the kinds of interventions and approaches that might help the missing groups, especially those whose life chances have been damaged by lack of skills and qualifications, to view education in a more positive light and benefit from the opportunities available.

This is not to imply that men (or women) who do not participate in formal, organised programmes of study are not 'learners' in the broad sense of the term. It is generally accepted that individuals learn continuously throughout their lives, experientially, incidentally or intentionally. Much of this learning is informal and unrecorded and does not take place in an educational institution. Nor is it implied that people who do not engage in organised learning programmes are any less talented, enterprising or resourceful than those who do. Individuals have a perfect right to exercise choice in the activities in which they engage. It is, however, a question of equity. If we have education and training programmes and institutions which are ostensibly open to all but which attract only certain segments of the population, then that 'openness' is itself open to question. Recent consultative papers and reports on lifelong learning and widening participation – Kennedy, 1997; Fryer, 1997; the National Committee of Enquiry into Higher Education, 1997 and the Green Paper, *The Learning Age* – all accept that some social groups, whether by choice, circumstance or the way the system is structured, fail to benefit from organised education and training opportunities. To varying degrees these publications also accept the notion that individuals in these groups may be learning in other, equally valid, though formally unrecognised ways, outside of institutions. However, the general message is that if we aspire to be a learning society with a culture of lifelong learning, the problem of unequal access to education and training opportunities needs to be addressed.

If certain groups of men are not coming forward, why not? Is it a simple matter of choosing to spend their time in other ways or is there a fundamental mismatch between formal education and some aspects of male culture? Does the ethos of education and training institutions and centres, and the way in which learning programmes are presented, militate against the participation of certain male groups? Are there clear differences between male and female patterns of participation? Do approaches that have worked effectively with women also work with men? These are some of the questions that the following study sets out to explore. It is organised as follows:

- The context: participation patterns of men and women
- The implications: why we should be concerned about the 'missing' groups
- Understanding male attitudes and participation patterns
- Young men: examples of approaches to improve motivation and participation
- Men over 25: examples of approaches to improve motivation and participation
- Conclusions

Table 1. Population distribution by gender and age group, 1995

Great Britain	57 millions			
Age group	Females (thousands)	% of total population	Males (thousands)	% of total population
Under 16	5,694	10	5,994	11
16–19	1,272	2	1,349	2
20–29	4,086	7	4,276	8
30–49	8,127	14	8,252	14
50–64	4,497	8	4,394	8
65 and over	5,358	9	3,656	6
Working age (16–59/64)	16,592	29	18,272	32
All ages	29,035	51	27,922	49

Source: Office for National Statistics

CHAPTER ONE

The context: participation patterns of men and women

The first issue to be explored is whether there are significant variations between men and women in their levels and patterns of participation in post-compulsory education and training.

Social class differences

There are some general trends, confirmed with monotonous regularity in survey after survey, regarding the determinants of adult participation in learning, although the actual numbers of participants fluctuate according to the questions asked. Surveys consistently show that the most significant predictors of individual involvement in post-school learning are school-leaving age, the holding of school qualifications, age and occupational status. The National Adult Learning Survey (NALS) which was conducted in England and Wales in 1997 (SCPR, 1997) was more inclusive in its definition of learning than most surveys. It covered both taught learning activities (courses leading to qualifications or job skills; evening classes; instruction in practical skills, use of study materials and other courses or tuition) and self-directed, untaught learning activities not involving courses (studying for qualifications; supervised, on-the-job training; keeping skills up-to-date and improving knowledge).

The survey found that considerably more adults had engaged in learning since leaving full-time continuous education than suggested by other surveys which have employed a narrower definition of the term. In other respects it confirmed previous survey findings, by revealing that those most likely to have recently taken part in different types of learning activities were males, younger people, people in paid work, those working currently or formerly in managerial, professional or other non-manual occupations, and those who had stayed longer in continuous full-time education and gained higher qualifications. The groups least likely to have undertaken learning in the previous three years were people aged 50 and over (including those in retirement), those looking after the home or family, people unable to work because of long-term sickness and people who had left school at 16 or younger without qualifications (SCPR, 1997) (Table 2, see p13).

The NIACE/Gallup survey conducted for NIACE in 1996 (Sargant *et al*, 1997) also found the highest participation rates among the younger adult cohorts and those in occupational groups AB and C1; the lowest were among older adults and those in groups C2 (skilled manual) and DE unskilled/unemployed). About 60 per cent of those who had left school at age 18 were current or recent learners compared with 39 per cent of those who had left at 16-17 and 20 per cent of those who had left school before the age of 16.

National data on further education confirm that individuals from a manual working background are conspicuously under-represented in further education (DfE, 1993). Similarly, higher education data indicate that, despite the expansion of the sector, the overall social profile of students has not substantially changed: the majority still come from a middle class, and especially professional and managerial class, background. Although detailed social class data on mature students is not available, the existing evidence suggests a *'substantial under-representation of the skilled non-manual, skilled manual and partly skilled social classes' (HEFCE, 1996:23). As Robertson observes (1997:10): 'Universities have generally expanded participation within the same social segments as before (...) Where success can be measured — amongst adults and women for example — it has to be qualified by the recognition that high-prestige higher education remains available principally to white, middle-class, able-bodied young men (...)'.*

Gender differences in participation

Like the NIACE Gallup survey conducted a year or so earlier (Sargant et al, 1997), the 1997 National Adult Learning Survey found that more men than women had been recently involved in learning, although there were differences relating to age, economic activity and the type of learning engaged in. Some gender differences are already apparent at age 16.

Staying-on rates
The numbers of young people participating in post-school education have grown steadily in recent years. In 1997, 75 per cent of all 16-18 year olds were involved in education or training in England compared with 66 per cent of the cohort in 1991. The increase has been particularly marked for young women, a higher proportion of whom than of young men now engage in some form of education after age 16. The participation rate of women aged 18 and over has also been increasing rapidly. In England, between 1990 and 1995 it rose from 42 to 59 per cent, while that of men in the same age group increased from 50 to 60 per cent (EOC, 1997). Participation rates for this age group are now nearly equal for both sexes. Slightly more young men than young women are not involved in any form of education and training (Table 3, see p14). As the table shows, more women than men aged 16-18 continue in full- or part-time education while more male than female school-leavers participate in government- and employer-funded training. After age 20, there are slightly more male than female participants. In 1997, 15 per cent

of 20-24 year olds were involved in full-time education, of whom there were 34,000 more men than women (DfEE, 1998a and c).

Differences according to social and ethnic background

There are greater variations in participation patterns between groups from different social and ethnic backgrounds than between the sexes. Table 4 (see p15) shows that the highest proportion of 16-year-olds in full-time education in 1994 had parents in managerial, professional and other non-manual occupations. In each socio-economic group that year, an equal or higher proportion of women than men remained in post-compulsory education (DfEE, 1997e). The table also shows that a considerably higher proportion of members of minority ethnic groups continued in full-time education than members of the white population. In 1996, the gap between white people aged 16-24 and those from other ethnic backgrounds participating in full- or part-time education was over 15 per cent (Table 5, see p15). In contrast to white students, however, men from black ethnic minority groups tend to participate in greater numbers than women. Moreover the link between educational participation and social class is not as strong as it is within the white population. An analysis of 1991 census data (Karn, 1996) found that in six out of nine minority ethnic groups, participation rates amongst skilled worker households matched or exceeded those of the white professional and managerial group. There was also, unlike in the white population, a high participation rate among groups with partly skilled or unskilled heads of household. These differences have been attributed to several possible causes: a higher commitment to education among minority ethnic communities; the belief that qualifications provide the best route into the labour market, or a wish to delay entry to the labour market to avoid expected discrimination. In addition, many minority ethnic pupils are placed in low ability bands at school and therefore need to make up for their lack of GCSE passes after age 16 (Karn, 1996).

Location, type and mode of learning

Surveys of the whole adult population reveal some general differences in male and female learning preferences.

Adult and further education

Local education authority provision and community-based adult education courses, whether general, academic or vocational, continue to be heavily dominated by women (Table 6, see p16). In recent years, however, women have also been entering further and higher education in increasing numbers. They now outnumber men in both sectors, a trend that continues year on year. In 1997, the numbers of women participating in provision funded by the Further Education Funding Council (FEFC) exceeded those of male participants in all age groups, particularly those aged over 25 (Table 7, see p17). As the table shows, there are significant gender differences in modes of learning. Considerably more women than men enrol in part-time and evening-only further education programmes. They also outnumber men in open and distance programmes. In 1997-98, there were twice as many female as male enrolments with the National Extension College.

In general, women tend to take more varied and flexible qualification routes than men. In further education they are more likely than men to be studying for GNVQs, GCSEs and A or A/S levels while men are more often found on programmes leading to vocational qualifications. Women are also more likely than men to seek Open College Network (OCN) accreditation. Data for 1994-96 show that about twice as many women register on OCN accredited programmes as men, although nearly as many men as women receive additional learning support. In 1995-96, the majority of registrations were from learners who were unemployed or unwaged and about 13 per cent were from people belonging to minority ethnic communities (NOCN, 1996).

Higher education

In higher education, the number of women students has also increased significantly, as Chart 1 (see p16) and Table 8 (see p18) illustrate. It accelerated from 80,000 full-time undergraduates in 1975 to over 400,000 in 1995. Since 1995-96 women's enrolments have exceeded those of men on first degrees and other undergraduate courses, regardless of mode of attendance (although this is not the case for the Open University where there are slightly more male than female students). In 1996 there were 4,000 more female than male entrants to full-time degree programmes and 7,000 more female than male entrants to part-time degrees (although male first degree students are almost twice as likely as women to study for a higher degree by research (DfEE, 1997e)).

According to some, the changing gender balance disguises persisting inequalities since the number of women entering the sector has increased *more in the lower status – especially part-time – courses than in full-time courses* (Blackburn and Jarman, 1993: 210). Women are concentrated in fewer subject areas and often enter at a later age than men. Women are also more likely than men to enrol on Access courses and to enter higher education as mature students. In 1997, the majority of the 776,000 students aged over 25 in higher education institutions were women. Although provisional figures for mature entrants to full-time undergraduate courses since 1995 are showing an overall decline, this is apparently mainly related to a drop in male mature entrants: the number of female entrants has remained stable.

Minority ethnic groups are also disproportionately represented among mature students on first degree courses. In 1994-95 almost one in eight of all UK-domiciled students taking first degrees were from non-white ethnic groups, more than double their overall representation in the UK population. The largest group was Indian (27 per cent) and the smallest Bangladeshi

(3 per cent). The vast majority were aged over 21 and 50 per cent were over 25. Women were better represented than men among African-Caribbean, other black and Chinese groups (Connor *et al*, 1996; Barnard, 1997a).

Subject choice

There are some clear differences between the sexes in their choice of subjects. At A level, for example, considerably more men than women take mathematics, the physical sciences, technology, geography and computer studies while far more women than men choose English, modern foreign languages and social studies. Similarly, in further and higher education, male students are concentrated in the 'harder' physical sciences, engineering and technology subjects and women in arts, humanities and medical-related subjects (Tables 9 and 10, see pp18-19).

In the adult education sector, women tend to enrol in a wide range of general and self-development programmes whereas male learners are more restricted in their subject choices and, according to a former member of Her Majesty's Inspectorate: *'usually into IT, languages, sports, quasi mechanical stuff'*.

Although more women than men are involved in general, non-vocational learning, most adult learning surveys indicate the popularity with both sexes, but particularly with men, of practical subject areas such as computer studies, business and management skills, professional and vocational qualifications and modern foreign languages (Table 11, see p19). In the 1996 Gallup survey (Sargant *et al*, 1997), computer studies and foreign languages topped the list of subjects that both sexes, but again mostly men, would be interested in studying in the future.

Surveys suggest that among minority ethnic groups, both sexes prefer vocational subjects to arts subjects or 'leisure' learning activities. In this respect there are fewer differences between the sexes than between communities. One study (Sargant, 1993) found that English was important to people from the Indian subcontinent and for those from the Chinese communities while people of African origin preferred business management and administration. The most popular subject choices among the Caribbean women were business management, social work and community care, typing and word-processing. For Caribbean men the most popular choice was computer studies followed by engineering and social sciences. Among men from the Indian sub-continent the most popular courses were those leading to professional qualifications, English, foreign languages, computer studies and science (Sargant, 1993).

Dominant motivations

Generally speaking (though there will obviously be many exceptions), white British women tend more than men to engage in learning activities which are connected with self-development and which will expand their interests and activities and lead to educational progression. Men appear to be more single-minded, focused and practical in their motivation to learn, seeking to further specific goals or particular interests. The 1997 National Adult Learning Survey (SCPR, 1997) found that men, especially those in full-time employment, were more likely than women to have undertaken some self-directed, non-taught learning and to have engaged in learning for labour-market purposes. In the three years prior to the survey, 72 per cent of male learners had undertaken some vocational learning (defined as learning started to help with current or future work, whether paid or voluntary) and 27 per cent had been involved in non-vocational learning (defined as learning unrelated to work). For women, the percentages were 61 per cent and 32 per cent respectively. Men who had left full-time education without qualifications and those working full-time in manual occupations were the least likely to be involved in any form of non vocational learning.

In the NIACE/Gallup survey conducted in 1996, over 50 per cent of men gave work-related reasons for learning compared with 44 per cent of women. Although many women now have a strong career orientation, they are still more likely than men to have non-economic motivations in returning to learning (Clayton and Slowey, 1997).

Thus the evidence confirms that instrumental, work-related reasons are still the most dominant motives for learning among men, although they are also increasing for women as more of them enter the workforce. There are, however, some expected variations according to age. A study of male learners and non-learners conducted in North Yorkshire (North Yorkshire TEC, 1997) found that while young men and those under 50 were attending further education courses to achieve qualifications and improve job prospects, men over 50 were more likely to be attending out of personal interest and for personal satisfaction.

Work-related training

The greater tendency for men to be learning for reasons connected to employment is reflected in their scale of participation in work-related training. Whereas the numbers of women exceed those of men in post-compulsory education as a whole, more men than women participate in government- and employer-supported training. Among the younger cohorts, however, women are rapidly catching up.

Youth Training

In the early years of its operation, more young men than young women took part in the Youth Training (YT) programme, but by the end of 1997, there were almost as many women joining the programme as men, with people from minority ethnic groups composing about 6-7 per cent of total participants (DfEE 1997a). The programme strongly reflects sex divisions in the labour market with the majority of male and female trainees training in traditional male or female occupational areas (EOC, 1997).

Similar divisions characterise the Modern Apprenticeship scheme (MAPPs). This was launched in 1994 with the aim of increasing the number of young people achieving NVQ level 3 and initially attracted a majority of young men training in traditionally male-dominated industries such as engineering, manufacturing, construction and the motor industry. By the middle of 1996, however, almost half of the 41,000 apprentices were women training mainly in stereotypical female areas such as child care, health and social care, hairdressing and business administration. There was a greater gender balance in some occupational sectors, notably retailing, hotel and catering, accountancy, sports and recreation (Table 12, see p19).

Training for Work

Twice as many men as women have been involved in the Training for Work programme where they currently compose about 70 per cent of participants. Despite being in a minority on the programme and slightly less likely than men to gain a qualification, women have been more successful than men in obtaining a job after leaving the programme. In 1997 the difference was 9-10 percentage points (DfEE 1997a) (Table 13, see p20).

Minority ethnic group participation

In the 12 months leading to September 1997, 85 per cent of entrants to Training for Work were white; 7 per cent were from black African Caribbean minority groups, 5 per cent from the Asian groups and 3 per cent from other ethnic groups (DfEE 1997a). These groups have been less well represented in the Youth Training programme. One analysis (Chatrik, 1997a) suggested that they are severely under-represented on mainstream youth training programmes but over-represented on preparation programmes which provide taster courses for those who have not gained Youth Training placements. In London, for example, 70-80 per cent of students taking preparation training are black but only about 30-40 per cent of mainstream trainees are black.

The number of black participants in MAPPs is also low. At the start of 1997, 3.4 per cent of trainees in England were from African, Caribbean and Asian communities and these were concentrated in a limited number of sectors – arts and entertainment, housing and telecommunications. Although the London region has a relatively high representation of young black people in the scheme, other areas with high black populations have a very low representation. It is suggested that employer resistance, social conditioning and inadequate qualifications may have contributed to this situation (Chatrik, 1997b) (Table 14, see p21).

Employer-supported training

Data from the National Child Development Study has revealed that men have: *'a substantially higher probability than women of undertaking employer provided and work-related training leading to a formal vocational qualification (both employer and non employer provided).'* (Dearden *et al*, 1997).

The findings of the 1996 NIACE/Gallup survey led to a similar conclusion (Sargant *et al*, 1997). This is in spite of the fact that participation in work-related training appears to be increasing faster for women than for men. For several years now, labour force surveys have shown that a slightly higher proportion of women than men received job-related training in the four weeks before the interview (Table 15, see p22). The table indicates that women in three occupational groups – managers and administrators; professionals, and associate professional and technical groups are more likely than men to have receive training. However, closer analysis of the data (Callender and Metcalf, 1997) suggests that the figures camouflage major differences in employment patterns and personal characteristics. The researchers argue that the fact that a greater proportion of women than men receive training can be explained by their concentration in industries and occupations which provide more training; by their shorter length of service with each employer, and by interacting factors such as age, qualifications and conditions of employment.

For both sexes the incidence of training decreases with age. But, whereas young men up to the age of 25 appear to receive more training than young women, after that age a higher proportion of women benefit from work-related training than men. Notably, women returning to work in their 30s and 40s tend to receive more training than men of the same age. (DfEE, 1997c). On the other hand, statistics for 1997 show that younger workers and male employees generally received longer training than female employees, so the situation is not as straightforward as the figures by themselves suggest. Women are also more likely than men to contribute towards the cost of their own training (Table 16, see p22). In spring 1996, over eight per cent more men than women had received employer funding for off-the-job training and over five per cent more women than men had funded their own off-the-job training (DfEE, 1997c).

Learning in later life

Some gender differences in patterns of participation are also apparent within the older (post-50) age cohorts. In Britain, as in the European Community as a whole, more older women than older men enrol in general education courses, although older men outnumber older women on courses leading to qualifications (EC, 1997). Typically, women outnumber men by about two to one in the University of the Third Age (U3A). This may be partly because there are more older women than older men in the population and many live alone. However, it may also be connected with the nature of U3A learning which tends to be informal and social in character (Midwinter, undated).

A British survey of students aged over 60 in all the main types of taught provision revealed some connections between the gender of students, their level of qualification and the type of provider frequented. Those with the lowest or no qualifications tended to be learning in local authority centres and institutions (over 70 per cent of these were women) while those with the highest qualifications (mainly men) tended to be involved in forms of distance learning. One of the most striking findings was that most of these learners were *continuing rather than embarking on an involvement in education* (Clennell, 1990). This is a characteristic of adult learners of all ages.

Learning in voluntary organisations

Some of the gender differences that characterise adult participation in learning are also apparent in patterns of involvement in voluntary organisations. In his study of the subject, Elsdon (1995) found that women had a higher rate of involvement in voluntary organisations than men and were more likely to join a generalist group. Men were more interested in specialist, single-interest organisations. Elsdon noted that there was some correlation between these trends and educational level. Individuals with minimum school experience, particularly men, were much more likely to be found in specialist organisations than those with longer first cycle education. Those whose education had been least privileged also tended (albeit with significant exceptions) to have a narrower range of interests that were more congruent with the voluntary organisation's objectives. His analysis revealed contrasting types of participative behaviour that varied according to gender. Members of specialist organisations (mainly men) usually had a moderate number of activities and interests which diminished to *a stable minimum* once they had joined the group which most effectively met their needs. Members of generalist groups, on the other hand, (mainly women), tended to discover new interests and gradually expand their range of activities beyond the group's immediate objectives. They also displayed: *evidence of intellectual and cultural adventurousness to a much higher degree than men, whose interests are more linear and focused, especially upon practical activities* (p44).

• • •

Overall, therefore, there are discernible differences in men's and women's patterns of participation in learning activities. Some of these, such as different subject choices and women's greater preference for general, self-developmental learning, have long been in evidence. Others, such as the rapid increase in the numbers of women enrolling in further and higher education programmes, are relatively recent developments. Men's overall rates of participation have not decreased: the 1996 NIACE/Gallup survey indicated that more men were planning to engage in learning than in the previous national survey undertaken in 1994. However, the sharp rise in the numbers of women engaging in organised education – presumably to make up for missed opportunities – makes this appear to be the case, as does the fact that men do not frequent as many learning environments and sectors as women. Men use vocational training and degree programmes as their main educational pathways to career and economic status, while women follow a wider range of learning routes to achieve greater societal and economic participation. They are more likely than men to be involved in non-vocational learning and far more likely than men to continue learning after age 40.

Non-learners

But what about the *non*-learners? Looking at participation data as a whole, men, like women, are unevenly represented in taught post-compulsory education and training although they participate overall in slightly greater numbers and are more likely than women to have had some experience of formal education or training since leaving school. As adult learning surveys consistently show, it is younger and employed men, especially those in higher level occupations and those who already have higher qualifications, who account for the greater incidence of male participation in learning. People who left school at age 16 or under and those with fewest skills and qualifications, are the least likely to be involved, and the least likely to want or expect to be involved, in organised learning programmes.

Current employment status is a particularly important predictor of participation: individuals who are in paid employment are more likely to be undertaking education and training than those who are not employed. In this respect, Britain compares badly with some other parts of Europe. A study of employment in Europe undertaken in 1996 found that 40 per cent more economically inactive men aged 25-34 were engaged in education and training programmes in Denmark, Germany, Austria and Sweden than in the UK (EC, 1996).

In this country many men, especially the long-term unemployed, manual workers, men with poor literacy and no or few qualifications, ex-offenders and African Caribbean, men are significantly under-represented in many forms of formal education and training provision. Whether this is a matter of personal choice or structural exclusion, these are groups who are particularly vulnerable to economic and social marginalisation and about whom we should be most concerned.

Table 2. Participation in learning by sex, age, activity status, occupation and household type

	% vocational learners	% non-vocational learners
Sex		
Males	72	27
Females	61	32
Age		
16-19	76	29
20-29	82	32
30-39	78	29
40-49	73	29
50-59	60	30
60-69	28	29
Activity Status		
In paid work	82	30
Unemployed	66	25
Looking after home and family	31	29
Retired	20	33
Long term sickness	23	28
Occupation (SEG)		
Professional/Managerial	85	34
Other non-manual	80	36
Skilled manual	65	24
Semi-skilled manual	64	23
Unskilled manual	44	19
Household type		
Single person	63	30
Partner, no child under 18	59	31
Partner and child under 18 present	73	29
Child under 18, no partner	59	27
Parent(s), no partner or child under 18	80	29

Source: *The National Adult Learning Survey, SCPR, 1997*

Table 3. Post-compulsory educational activities of 16-18 year olds,[1] 1996/97

England   Thousands and percentages

| AGE | At January 1997 | | | | | | | | | | | |
| | 16 | | | 17 | | | 18 | | | 16-18 | | |
	All	Males	Females	All	Males	Females	All	Males	Females	All	Males	Females
Population (Thousands)	619	318	301	604	310	293	557	286	270	1,780	915	865
In all education and training[2]	86.4	84.9	88.0	78.7	78.2	79.2	59.7	60.0	59.3	75.4	74.8	76.0
Full-time and part-time education	77.3	74.9	79.9	66.4	64.2	68.8	46.9	46.6	47.3	64.1	62.4	65.9
of which												
Schools[3]	33.9	32.4	35.4	26.2	25.0	27.5	3.1	3.3	2.9	21.7	20.8	22.6
Further Education[4]	43.5	42.5	44.5	39.6	38.7	40.7	23.4	24.1	22.6	35.9	35.4	36.4
Higher Education[4]	–	–	–	0.5	0.5	0.6	20.5	19.3	21.7	6.6	6.2	7.0
of which in full-time education	70.3	67.0	73.7	58.0	54.9	61.3	38.1	37.1	39.2	56.1	53.5	58.7
of which												
Schools[3]	33.9	32.4	35.4	26.2	25.0	27.5	3.1	3.3	2.9	21.7	20.8	22.6
Further Education[4]	36.4	34.6	38.3	31.3	29.5	33.2	15.1	15.2	14.9	28.0	26.8	29.3
Higher Education[4]	–	–	–	0.5	0.4	0.6	19.9	18.6	21.3	6.4	6.0	6.9
All Government Supported Training	10.1	11.4	8.7	11.5	13.5	9.4	8.6	10.1	7.0	10.1	11.7	8.4
of which												
On YT[5]	8.4	9.1	7.7	9.2	10.3	8.0	6.0	6.7	5.2	7.9	8.7	7.0
On Training for Work[5]	–	–	–	–	–	–	0.1	0.2	0.1	–	0.1	–
On Modern Apprenticeships[5]	1.6	2.3	1.0	2.3	3.3	1.4	2.5	3.3	1.6	2.1	2.9	1.3
Employer funded training[6]	2.0	3.0	1.1	3.3	3.9	2.7	4.5	5.4	3.5	3.2	4.1	2.4
Other education and training[7]	4.8	4.6	5.0	6.7	7.0	6.4	9.0	8.0	10.0	6.7	6.5	7.0
Not in any education or training	13.6	15.1	12.0	21.3	21.8	20.8	40.3	40.0	40.7	24.6	25.2	24.0

Source: Education and Training Statistics for the UK, 1997, Department for Education and Employment

[1] Age as at 31 August of the preceding year.

[2] Full and part-time education and training. Excludes overlap between education and Government Supported Training (GST).

[3] Includes maintained, independent and special schools.

[4] Students in public sector institutions except on Government Supported Training (GST) within colleges.

[5] Includes those in further education establishments attending GST courses.

[6] Includes young people in employment, eg non-GST apprentices and others on long and short term training programmes.

[7] Includes young people attending independent colleges and training centres, or at any college in part-time study not related to their job, or in part-time education but not currently employed.

Table 4. Participation rates[1] of 16 year olds in full-time education, England and Wales, 1994

Ethnic origin	Men	Women
White	67	74
Ethnic minority	88	84
Parents' Socio Economic Group		
Managerial/Professional	83	88
Other non-manual	82	85
Skilled manual	63	72
Semi-skilled manual	56	66
Unskilled manual	56	56
Other/not classified	60	63

Source: YCS cohort 7, Sweep 1 (Separate Tables, DfEE, 1997)

[1] Percentage of the group defined at each row whose main activity was full time education

Table 5. Percentage of 16-24 age group in education[1]

Per cent

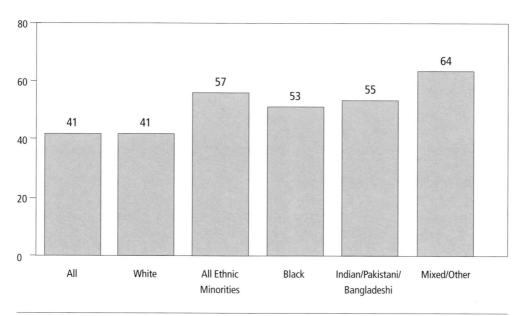

Source: Labour Force Survey, Spring 1996

[1] Percentage of the group in full- or part-time education

Table 6. Enrolments on adult education centre courses: by type of course, gender and age, 1994/95

England and Wales							Thousands
	Academic		Vocational		Other[1]		All enrolments
	Males	Females	Males	Females	Males	Females	
16-18	2.9	4.9	1.3	4.8	15.4	22.4	51.7
19 and over	17.6	44.5	31.0	97.9	231.9	641.4	1,064.3
All aged 16 and over	20.5	49.4	32.3	102.7	247.3	663.8	1,116.0

Source: Department for Education and Employment; Welsh Office

[1] Includes those on Basic Education and General Education courses (that is, languages, physical education/sport/fitness, practical craft/skills, role education, other adult education)

Chart 1. Students in higher education, 1975/76-1993/94

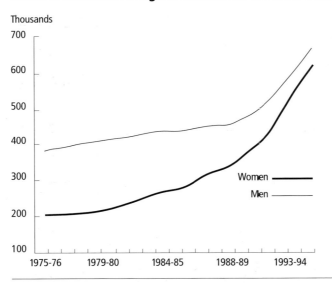

Sources: University Grants Committee, Universities' Statistical Record, Department for Education and Employment, Welsh Office

Table 7. Students (in 000s) enrolled on council-funded provision in further education sector colleges in England on 1 November 1997 by age and sex and by college type and mode of attendance

College type	Mode of attendance	Under 16			16-18			19-20			21-24			25-59			60 and over		
		Female	Male	All	Female	Male	All	Female	Male	All	Female	Male	All	Female	Male	All	Female	Male	All
General FE and tertiary colleges	Full-time full-year	0.5	0.7	1.2	177.4	167.5	344.9	18.0	21.2	39.2	16.9	15.2	32.1	64.1	37.0	101.1	0.9	1.1	2.0
	Other full-time	–	–	–	1.9	2.2	4.1	1.0	0.9	1.9	1.9	1.6	3.5	10.0	6.8	16.8	0.2	0.2	0.4
	Part time	1.8	1.5	3.3	50.6	53.9	104.5	34.0	32.0	66.0	79.1	56.5	135.6	539.4	344.2	883.6	33.6	26.6	60.2
	of which evening only	1.0	0.5	1.5	18.7	10.8	29.6	14.2	8.7	22.9	36.4	21.0	57.3	221.5	142.2	363.8	8.7	10.1	18.8
	of which open/distance	0.1	–	0.1	2.9	1.7	4.6	2.8	1.6	4.3	6.6	3.7	10.3	40.9	28.3	69.2	1.0	1.3	2.3
	Total	**2.3**	**2.2**	**4.6**	**222.9**	**223.6**	**453.5**	**52.9**	**54.1**	**107.0**	**97.9**	**73.3**	**171.2**	**613.5**	**388.0**	**1,001.5**	**34.6**	**28.0**	**62.6**
Sixth form colleges	Full-time full-year	0.2	0.1	0.3	59.4	51.3	110.7	0.7	0.9	1.7	0.2	0.2	0.4	0.9	0.2	1.2	–	–	–
	Other full-time	–	–	–	0.1	–	0.1	–	–	–	–	–	–	0.1	0.1	0.2	–	–	–
	Part time	0.1	–	0.1	2.3	2.0	4.3	0.9	0.6	1.5	1.8	0.9	2.7	15.6	6.8	22.5	0.9	1.0	1.9
	of which evening only	0.1	–	0.1	0.8	0.4	1.2	0.6	0.3	0.8	1.2	0.5	1.7	9.7	4.4	14.0	0.5	0.6	1.1
	of which open/distance	–	–	–	–	–	–	–	–	–	0.1	–	0.1	0.3	0.2	0.4	–	–	–
	Total	**0.3**	**0.1**	**0.4**	**61.8**	**53.3**	**115.5**	**1.7**	**1.5**	**3.2**	**2.1**	**1.1**	**3.1**	**16.7**	**7.1**	**23.8**	**1.0**	**1.0**	**2.0**
Other colleges	Full-time full-year	–	–	–	5.2	6.0	11.3	0.6	1.1	1.7	0.3	0.6	0.9	1.1	1.2	2.3	–	–	–
	Other full-time	–	–	–	–	–	–	–	–	0.1	–	–	0.1	0.1	0.1	0.2	–	–	–
	Part time	–	–	–	0.7	1.3	2.0	0.4	0.6	0.9	0.7	0.8	1.5	8.6	5.6	14.2	0.6	0.4	1.1
	of which evening only	–	–	–	0.1	–	0.1	0.1	0.1	0.1	0.2	0.1	0.3	2.1	1.5	3.5	0.1	0.1	0.2
	of which open/distance	–	–	–	–	0.1	0.1	–	–	0.1	0.1	0.1	0.2	0.6	0.8	1.4	–	–	–
	Total	**–**	**–**	**0.1**	**5.9**	**7.3**	**13.3**	**1.0**	**1.7**	**2.7**	**1.1**	**1.4**	**2.5**	**9.8**	**6.9**	**16.7**	**0.7**	**0.4**	**1.1**
Total all colleges	Full-time full-year	0.7	0.8	1.5	242.0	224.9	466.9	19.3	23.3	42.6	17.4	16.0	33.4	66.1	38.4	104.5	0.9	1.2	2.1
	Other full-time	–	–	–	2.0	2.2	4.2	1.0	0.9	2.0	2.0	1.6	3.6	10.2	6.9	17.1	0.2	0.2	0.4
	Part time	1.9	1.6	3.5	53.6	57.2	110.8	35.3	33.2	68.4	81.6	58.2	139.8	563.7	356.7	920.4	35.2	28.0	63.2
	of which evening only	1.0	0.6	1.6	19.6	11.3	30.9	14.8	9.0	23.9	37.7	21.6	59.3	233.3	148.1	381.3	9.2	10.8	20.0
	of which open/distance	0.1	–	0.1	2.9	1.8	4.7	2.8	1.6	4.5	6.8	3.9	10.6	41.7	29.3	71.0	1.0	1.4	2.4
	Total	**2.6**	**2.4**	**5.0**	**297.6**	**284.3**	**581.9**	**55.6**	**57.4**	**112.9**	**101.0**	**75.8**	**176.9**	**639.9**	**402.0**	**1,042.0**	**36.2**	**29.4**	**65.6**
% students		0.1	0.1	0.3	14.9	14.2	29.1	2.8	2.9	5.6	5.1	3.8	8.8	32.0	20.1	52.1	1.8	1.5	3.3

Source: Statistics for enrolment on council-funded provision for November 1997, FEFC

Table 8. Enrolments in higher education by gender, mode of attendance and level of course, United Kingdom, 1980/81-1994/95

All enrolments (home and overseas)   Thousands

		Full-time				Part-time		
		Open University[2]	Under-graduate[1]	Post-graduate	Total[4]	Under-graduate[1]	Post-graduate	Total[4]
1980-81	Men	38	277	41	318	140	29	169
	Women	29	196	21	217	44	11	56
1985-86	Men	43	294	44	339	139	34	172
	Women	36	237	24	261	70	16	86
1990-91	Men	43	344	50	339	148	45	193
	Women	36	318	33	352	106	32	138
1992-93	Men	53	436	61	496	150	59	208
	Women	52	416	44	461	125	47	172
1993-94	Men	56	483	67	549	148	66	213
	Women	55	465	49	515	135	56	191
1994-95[3]	Men	62	509	74	582	149	71	221
	Women	57	505	56	561	151	66	217

Source: Further and Higher Education, UK Volume, 1995

[1] 'Undergraduate' includes first diplomas and certificates
[2] Includes associate and postgraduate students
[3] Provisional
[4] Total does not include Open University students

Table 9. Students in further education, 1994/95

Home students – United Kingdom   Thousands

	Females		Males	
Subject Group	Thousands	% Female	Thousands	% Male
Medicine, dentistry & allied studies	93.9	89	11.6	11
Agriculture	20.0	49	21.0	51
Mathematical science	75.4	51	73.1	49
Engineering & technology	15.8	8	185.5	92
Architecture	5.9	7	79.0	93
Social sciences	60.8	80	15.2	20
Business & financial	269.8	68	126.8	32
Languages	102.9	60	67.9	40
Creative arts	194.5	73	73.5	27
Education	52.5	63	30.7	37
All subjects*	1,457.9	57	1,083.5	43

Source: Department for Education and Employment

* Including those not listed separately

Table 10. Students in higher education, 1995/96

United Kingdom   Thousands

Subject Group	Undergraduates		Postgraduates	
	Females	Males	Females	Males
Medicine, dentistry & allied studies	93.6	30.2	15.8	10.4
Biological sciences	34.7	23.1	7.8	7.1
Physical sciences	20.5	36.1	5.0	12.0
Mathematical sciences	6.1	10.0	1.1	2.8
Engineering & technology	15.1	95.9	3.8	23.5
Social, economic & political studies	56.4	38.8	16.5	15.1
Business & administrative studies	78.7	77.4	21.6	37.4
Languages	52.1	22.6	7.5	5.3
All subjects*	**683.5**	**625.3**	**159.4**	**191.2**

Source: Higher Education Statistics Agency

* Including those not listed separately

Table 11. Subjects studied by men and women, United Kingdom

	Men	Women
	%	%
Computer Studies	18	15
Business/management	14	9
Other professional qualifications	11	12
Other vocational qualifications	9	10
Foreign languages	8	8
Nursing/health studies	5	11
Social sciences	5	7
Engineering	7	1
Social work/Community care	2	6
Other	21	21

Source: NIACE/Gallup Survey, 1996. Subjects of study by all current/recent learners

Table 12. Modern Apprenticeship start-ups, selected sectors, 1995-96

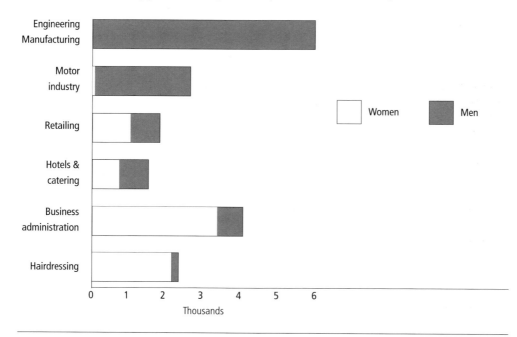

Source: Department for Education and Employment

Table 13. Training for work – composition of participants, September 1996- September 1997

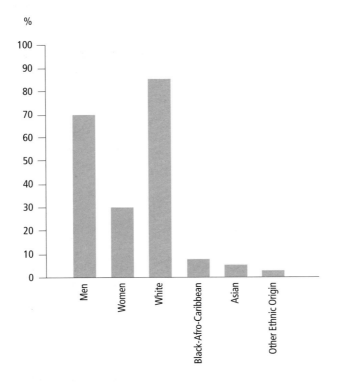

Table 14. Post-compulsory education and training: students and starters
Youth training[1] and Modern Apprenticeships[2]: characteristics of starts–time series

England and Wales								Percentage
	1990-91	1994-95[2]	1995-96[2]	1996-97	Apr-Jun 1996	Jul-Sep 1996	Oct-Dec 1996	Jan-Mar 1997
Youth Training[1]								
As a percentage of all starters								
Gender								
Males	59	56	53	51	50	53	50	51
Females	41	44	47	49	50	47	50	49
Age								
16	---	39	37	35	33	45	28	21
17	---	27	24	24	24	21	26	30
18	---	9	9	9	8	9	10	11
19+	---	22	27	29	29	21	35	38
Ethnic Origin								
White	92	93	93	93	94	94	94	92
Black/African/Caribbean	2	2	2	2	2	2	2	3
Indian/Pakistani/Bangladeshi/ Sri Lankan	3	3	3	3	3	3	3	4
Other	1	1	2	1	1	1	1	1
Special needs								
People with disabilities	4	5	5	6	7	6	6	6
Literacy/numeracy needs	---	5	6	7	8	6	6	7
English/Welsh/Gaelic for speakers of other languages	1	1	1	1	1	1	1	1
Modern Apprenticeships[2]								
As a percentage of all starters								
Gender								
Males	---	---	67	55	49	62	53	46
Females	---	---	33	45	51	38	47	54
Age								
16	---	---	23	19	12	29	16	9
17	---	---	24	18	19	19	18	17
18	---	---	20	18	19	19	17	17
over 18	---	---	33	45	50	34	48	56
Ethnic Origin								
White	---	---	97	96	96	97	96	95
Black/African/Caribbean	---	---	1	1	1	1	2	2
Indian/Pakistani/Bangladeshi/Sri Lankan	---	---	1	2	1	1	2	2
Other	---	---	1	1	1	1	1	1
Special needs								
People with disabilities	---	---	2	3	4	3	3	3
Literacy/numeracy needs	---	---	---	---	---	---	---	---
English/Welsh/Gaelic for speakers of other languages	---	---	---	---	---	---	---	---

Source: Department for Education and Employment

[1] Including Youth Credits
[2] Modern Apprenticeships was launched in September 1995, although some sectors operated prototypes from September 1994

Table 15. Proportion of employees of working age receiving job-related training during the last four weeks, Great Britain, Spring 1996

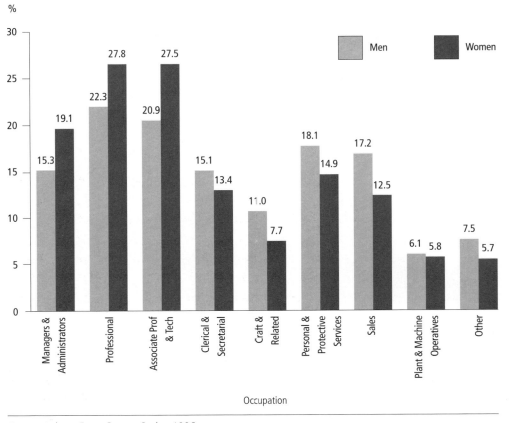

Source: Labour Force Survey, Spring 1996

Table 16. Source of fees for employees' off-the-job training, Great Britain, Spring 1996

	As a percentage of all off-the-job trainees	
	Men	Women
	%	%
Employer or potential employer	68.0	59.6
Government or Local Authority	12.8	16.3
Self, family or relative	15.7	21.1
Other	2.0	1.6
No fees	5.2	5.1

Source: Labour Force Survey, Spring 1996

[1] Employees of working age only: men aged 16 to 64 and women aged 16 to 59

[2] Includes those receiving off-the-job training only and those receiving both on and off-the-job training during the last four weeks

[3] Percentages sum to more than 100 per cent since some trainees received funding from more than one source

CHAPTER TWO

The implications: why we should be concerned about the 'missing' groups

Survey findings show that men with low literacy levels, no or few qualifications or skills and a history of unemployment are under-represented in all types of education and training provision, as indeed are women with these characteristics. However, it is timely to examine the reasons for the absence of certain groups of men from organised education and training especially as this has, up to now, been a relatively neglected area of research. Is there a link, for example, between adult male participation patterns and boys' underachievement at school?

Gender gap in school performance

The widening gap between male and female performance at key stages of compulsory education has been arousing increasing concern. National Curriculum Assessments at the three key stages (ages 7, 11 and 14) regularly show that girls outperform boys in English. At ages 7 and 11, there is already a marked difference between boys and girls in reading and writing ability. At age 11, girls also perform slightly better than boys in mathematics. The gap continues at subsequent test stages. In the 1997 National Curriculum Assessments of 14-year-olds in England, girls did considerably better than boys in English and mathematics.

Girls gain more GCSEs at all grades than boys and the gap between the numbers who gain five or more grades A* to C widened from 0.9 per cent in 1983-84 to 9.5 per cent in 1995-96 (DfEE, 1997c and e) (Table 17, see p42). Average points scores in 1997 were 39.2 for girls and 34.7 for boys.

Table 18 (see p43) shows the gender differences in GCSE/Standard grade results across subjects in England, Wales and Scotland. These are again particularly great in English. Results for 1997 showed that 43 per cent of boys achieved grade C or above in English compared with 65 per cent of girls (QCA, 1998).

The attainment gap is compounded by other factors: boys outnumber girls by two to one in schools for children with learning difficulties (Lloyd and Wood, 1996). They also have considerably higher levels of truancy and exclusion from school than girls. For the school year 1993-1994, 83 per cent of all permanent school exclusions and over 90 per cent of those excluded from primary schools were boys (DfEE, 1997c). Many of the boys excluded are black – African-Caribbean boys are four times more likely to be excluded from school than white boys (Lloyd and Wood, 1996).

The academic gap between girls and boys up to the age of 16 is not peculiar to Britain. A UNESCO-funded study (Gipps and Murphy, 1997) revealed that the same trend has emerged over the last few years in Australia, the US and Finland as well as in a range of developing countries. The study also revealed that boys have been behaving in an increasingly aggressive manner towards girls in many of these countries.

In this country, concern about boys' underachievement has led to action at national level. In his Fourth Annual Report, the Chief Inspector of Schools identified addressing boys' educational attainment levels as a priority and, early in 1998, School Standards Minister, Stephen Byers launched a coordinated raft of measures with the announcement: *We must challenge the laddish anti-learning culture which has been allowed to develop over recent years and not simply accept with a shrug of our shoulders that boys will be boys'* (DfEE Press Release 002/98). The measures included a requirement that each local education authority address the issue in its Education Development Plan; a commissioned report from the Qualifications and Curriculum Authority (QCA) on methods of raising boys' achievement in English across all ages and stages of schooling (QCA, 1998), and the commissioning of special research on boys' school performance from Homerton College and the University of Cambridge.

Some educationists believe that these reactions have been unduly alarmist. It is argued that girls' progress should be seen as part of a broader process of social change, and that there has been an over-simplistic interpretation of test and examination results: the difference in academic performance needs to be seen in the context of a general increase in levels of attainment for both sexes, albeit one that has been faster and more marked for girls than for boys. This has been attributed to a variety of causes: girls' more cooperative and positive attitudes to school, and increasing opportunities for women in the workplace and public life (*'parity in opportunities for adults yields parity in preparatory performances'* (Baker and Jones, 1993: 99)). Other causes have been identified as curriculum changes; an increased stress on literacy skills and verbal reasoning which girls acquire more rapidly than boys, and the adoption of teaching approaches, learning styles and assessment methods that particularly favour girls (Gallagher, 1997; Murphy and Elwood, 1996; Pyke, 1996).

Many attribute the disparities in examination results to changes in assessment procedures. It has been found that boys perform better in multiple-choice tests and practical activities while girls perform better at course work and essays. Gallagher (1997) cites a review of research evidence suggesting that boys and girls also deal differently with curriculum content and express themselves differently in written responses. This can affect assessment outcomes at successive stages of the education process:

'Certain styles of expression are expected in particular subject areas and thus influence teachers' judgements of students' ability often in ways that misrepresent their real

achievements. While girls appear to be advantaged by this in English, research indicates that the reverse obtains in science. Furthermore as students progress beyond compulsory education to GCE A Level study post-16 a shift in performance patterns arise that can again be seen to link to styles of response' (Murphy and Elwood, 1996: 17).

It is suggested that boys' and girls' choice of GCSE options also has a bearing on examination results. In science, for example, more boys than girls are entered for the double award option and the 'elite' single science subjects. Bell (1998) found that when the different entry patterns are taken into account, gender-related scores can be seen in a different light. His analysis indicated that girls still *under*achieve in the physical sciences and are not outstripping boys as a simple interpretation of results suggests.

Ireson (1998) attributes some of the gender disparities in achievement to setting by ability, arguing that low ability groups tend to include disproportionate numbers of boys, pupils from lower socio-economic groups, minority ethnic groups and those born in the summer.

Some claim that school performance is more strongly connected with social and economic background than with gender and that there are greater differences in achievement between groups within either sex than between the sexes as a whole. Plummer (1998) argues that the link between social class and educational attainment emerges as early as the infant school: it is already evident in National Curriculum test results for 7-year-olds and intensifies as children progress through school. She believes that the current concern about boys' underachievement is deflecting attention from the fact that girls from a working class background also significantly underachieve, albeit to a slightly lesser extent than boys: *'Analysis of external examinations at all ages show that working class underachievement is the real issue. The gap is particularly noticeable post 16. The sharp increase in the number of young people staying on after 16 helps to disguise that it is those from poorer areas who are still much more likely to leave without qualification. (...) Among the working classes higher education remains an exceptional experience'* (Plummer, 1998).

There is certainly evidence of a strong correlation between school attainment and poverty. An OFSTED chart based on 2,500 schools clearly demonstrates that those with the largest number of children receiving free school meals have the lowest GCSE scores (Table 19, see p43).

Thus opinions differ on the magnitude and gravity of the gender gap and warnings about over-reaction to the *'apparent underachievement of boys'* have been sounded in a report for the Department of Education Northern Ireland: *'With attainment patterns we need to be clear on what is being measured, how it is being measured and who is being measured. (...) Different types of examination or assessment systems can offer different gender patterns in attainment levels. Measured attainment levels based on a single criterion can incorporate gender biases reflecting socialisation patterns and opportunities to learn. For all these reasons gender differences in educational achievement are complex and do not lie in a single simple direction'* (Gallagher (1997: 39).

In another report from Northern Ireland similar caution is urged with regard to attainment levels post-16: *'Caution should be exercised in drawing oversimplified conclusions from attainment data, particularly where these relate to examination and assessment systems in post-compulsory education where not only the measured level of achievement, but also the comparative levels of participation need to be considered'* (DENI, 1997).

Post-compulsory attainment levels

The gender gap in academic achievement does not seem to be replicated after age 16 nor is it evident in vocational education.

In post-compulsory education and training, gender differences are more apparent in the nature, scale and patterns of participation, particularly at different ages, than in levels of achievement. In both further and higher education, there are greater differences between the sexes in the areas they choose to study than in their respective academic performance.

Data from Individualised Student Records for 1994-95 show that the attainment levels of women attending FEFC-funded, full-time provision are higher at all ages than those of men. However, among part-time students aged 18 upwards, slightly more men than women achieve full or partial qualifications (Table 20, see p44). More women than men are entered for and pass GCE AS/A level examinations and although, slightly more women achieve one or more passes at AS/A level (a gap of about six percentage points in 1994-95), the achievement of pass rates A to E are broadly similar for both sexes. As already noted, the most marked differences are in choice of subject: almost twice as many female as male entrants take arts subjects whereas far more boys than girls are entered for chemistry, physics, mathematics, craft, design and technology, and computer studies (Table 21, see p45).

In higher education, more women than men obtained first degrees during the academic year 1995-96 and a higher proportion of women than men obtained either first or second class degrees. However, the number of men obtaining a first class degree was slightly higher than that of women (DfEE, 1997c) (Table 22, see p46).

Training programmes

Data from government training programmes also show differences between the sexes in the occupational areas they enter, but relatively small differences in achievement level. In Youth Training, women and men gain qualifications and find jobs at about the same rate, although women are slightly less likely than men to complete their training. There are, however, differences in outcome for different population groups: leavers from minority ethnic groups have been 'consistently' less likely than white trainees to gain a job after leaving or to gain a qualification. Trainees with disabilities, literacy or numeracy needs and English or Welsh as a second language have also been less likely than others to complete training, gain qualifications and find a job on leaving. (DfEE, 1997a) (Table 23, see p46).

Follow-up surveys of Training for Work participants similarly show little difference between men and women in their completion rates and achievement of qualifications although a higher proportion of women than men gain a job after participating. Again, the main differences are between white and other groups: black African and Caribbean leavers are least likely to be in a job despite having similar completion and qualification rates to others (DfEEb; Donnelly, 1997-98) (Table 24, see p47).

There are some general differences in qualification levels between different racial and social groups. An analysis of 1991 census data (Karn, 1996) revealed significant variations in achievement between groups from different ethnic backgrounds: the highest qualified groups were the black African, Chinese, other Asian and 'other' groups, followed by the Indians and whites. The lowest qualified groups were black Caribbean, other black, Pakistani and Bangladeshi groups – *the same groups that other studies have shown to have poor school-level educational qualifications*.

Gender differences in qualifications held

Men are, as a whole, more highly qualified than women. More men than women of working age have qualifications at NVQ levels 3, 4 and 5 or equivalent with the widest gap emerging at level 3: 22 per cent of men have qualifications at this level but only 10 per cent of women – a situation that would seem to warrant concern equal to that about boys' underachievement at school. At level 2 there is little difference between the sexes but below this level the situation changes: 26 per cent of women have qualifications below level 2 compared with 18 per cent of men.

Data from 1997 labour force surveys also show that more women (21 per cent) than men (16 per cent) have no qualifications. The difference is less marked among the younger adult cohorts: women aged 40-59 are more likely to have no qualifications than men of the same age (Government Statistical Service, 1998) (Table 25, see p48).

The consequences of poor school performance

While it is clear that the disparities in gender performance at school do not extend to post-compulsory education, it would be wrong to conclude that there is not a problem for some boys. A number of young people annually drop out of school without achieving any qualifications and do not subsequently enter any form of education or employment. The majority of these – nearly 30,000 a year – are boys, For some, this may be fatal to their future prospects: *'Many of the teenagers who leave school without qualifications persist in their failure. One in five 17 year olds is in neither education nor training; nearly one third of FE students lacks basic literacy and numeracy, more than a half of those on youth training schemes fail to obtain a qualification'* (Williams, 1997a).

As suggested earlier, one of the characteristics of this group is their social class. In 1996, the Chief Inspector of OFSTED, Chris Woodhead, referred to the failure of boys, and *'particularly white working-class boys'*, as *'one of the most disturbing problems we face within the whole educational system'* (cited by Pyke, 1996). Since boys from African Caribbean backgrounds are among the lowest achievers as well as the most excluded from school, they should be included in this concern.

The 1996 OFSTED report concluded that African-Caribbean young people, especially boys, had not shared equally in increasing rates of achievement. In some areas their performance had worsened, even when differences in qualifications, social class and gender were taken into account. Minority ethnic boys suffer from what Karn (1996) describes as a ethnic penalty: as they tend to live in deprived areas they often lack access to the best schools. Their levels of educational attainment are then likely to be affected by discrimination within the education system (they are often placed in low ability bands and non-examination tracks and have the highest rates of school exclusion), as well as by discrimination in employment (the expectation of which is likely to affect educational aspirations and expectations).

The poor academic performance of boys in lower socio-economic groups is nothing new, but so long as there has been a continuing supply of unskilled jobs for them to take on leaving school, it has not been considered a huge problem. In today's world, however, poor achievement at school can have a stream of negative consequences: *'Lack of success in gaining qualifications at school shows up almost immediately as very early adult and social marginalisation'* (Mid Glamorgan TEC, 1996).

The link between low educational attainment and offending behaviour

Low school achievement often goes together with truanting, school exclusion and offending behaviour. Young men who cannot get an income from work or welfare benefits frequently seek money and stimulation by other means. Over 40 per cent of all offenders of school age who are sentenced in the youth court have been excluded from school, and a further 23 per cent truant significantly. Twenty per cent have a statement of special educational needs compared with 2-3 per cent of all secondary school children (Audit Commission, 1996).

Although there has been an apparent fall in youth crime since 1985 (attributed partly to a fall in the numbers of young people aged 10-20 in the population), a disproportionate amount of crime is still committed by young males who account for well over 80 per cent of indictable offences committed by those aged under 21. The 1991 National Prisoners' Survey found that 45 per cent of prisoners had left school before the age of 16 with one per cent never having attended school at all. Similarly, a study undertaken for the Audit Commission (1996) found that 60 per cent of a sample of young offenders on supervision orders were not engaged in work, training or education and many had difficulty with reading and writing. Whereas one in six of the general population has literacy problems, in the prison population this increases to one in two.

Males first convicted in their early teens are more likely to continue offending than those convicted later (Government Statistical Service, 1990). Analysis of American longitudinal data on men now in their mid-30s suggests that teenage boys who are convicted for drug offences and acts of violence pay a massive price in terms of their future social and economic status (Burgess and Propper, 1998).

The link between low educational attainment and social and economic disadvantage

Research has identified a growing gap between people who are *'getting on'*, those who are *'getting by'* and those who are *'getting nowhere'* – a group *'with neither the personal resources nor the skills to even get into the game'* (Bynner, Ferri and Shephard, 1997: 2). This can result from a cycle of disadvantage that starts in childhood. The National Child Development Study, which is following the changing circumstances of a sample of people born in 1958, has found that children from deprived family backgrounds tend to have lower educational attainment than those from better-off families. It also found that it is more difficult for men with poor qualifications and disadvantaged childhood circumstances to improve their prospects in adulthood than for women who have been similarly disadvantaged (Young, 1997).

According to a number of reports, the prospects for children in local authority care are particularly bleak. Over 40 per cent are not entered for GCSEs and up to 75 per cent leave school with no formal qualifications. The proportion without qualifications is high among those leaving residential care and those who experienced frequent moves (Audit Commission, 1996). After they leave school, the pattern of educational underachievement and social marginalisation continues: *'Fewer than 20 per cent go on to FE compared with 68 per cent of the general population. 30 per cent of homeless 16-17 year olds are care leavers as are 23 per cent of the adult prison population. They are also far more likely to be unemployed'* (Russell, 1997).

Many of those who drop out of school at or before age 16 have poor basic skills. The Basic Skills Agency has found that about 20 per cent of 21-year-olds are at or below foundation level in literacy, and even more have low levels of numeracy. These people are five times more likely to be unemployed as those who have good basic skills (Wells, 1997). Data from the National Child Development Study indicates that poor basic skills have an overwhelmingly negative impact on individuals as they progress through adult life. Women with poor basic skills tend to leave the labour market early and men are concentrated in low skilled, low paid areas of the labour market and vulnerable to successive periods of unemployment (Bynner and Parsons, 1997).

The link between low educational attainment and unemployment

The employment changes that have taken place over the last few decades have had a significant impact on both sexes, but particularly on men. Whereas women's labour market participation rate has been increasing, men's has been declining. Since 1976, the number of women in the labour force has increased by over 26 per cent and women now account for nearly half of the employed labour force. Male participation rates have fallen since 1990 and are expected to go on declining. In spring 1997 there were over 700,000 fewer employed men than there were at the beginning of the 1990s. Analysis of the spring 1995 Labour Force Survey showed that almost two thirds of people made redundant were men (DfEE, 1996). Female employment (albeit often temporary, part-time and low-paid) has overtaken male employment for all age groups. Young women and those leaving education and training schemes currently have a greater chance of getting jobs than their male counterparts. In the case of graduates the difference is 2 per cent. In the case of the Youth Training and Training for Work programmes the difference is around 1-2 percentage points and 10-11 percentage points respectively (DfEE, 1997b).

Although the British labour force has increased since the end of the last recession, its composition has changed. Between December 1992 and December 1996, 59 per cent of all new jobs were part-time and taken by women. Less than one in six was a full-time, male post. (Convery, 1997c). While there has been an increase in the number of full-time jobs for men since then, part-time work has continued to rise. Part-time workers now total around 7.4 million, over three quarters of whom are women (DfEE, 1998c).

The slow recovery of male employment can be attributed in part to the shift from full-time to part-time work, the decline of manufacturing jobs and the growth of the service sector in which women are disproportionately represented. These shifts have inevitably affected occupational patterns – white collar managerial and professional jobs have grown whilst manual jobs have declined. The greatest decline in male employment has occurred in manufacturing where there has been a loss of three and a half million jobs, the majority of which were held by men (EOC, 1997) (Table 26, see p48).

Nevertheless, according to labour force survey measures, unemployment has been steadily falling in the last few years. One of the biggest recorded reductions was in autumn 1997 leading to an overall (official) unemployment rate of 6.6 per cent. This is partly attributed to the unexpectedly high numbers of students entering education in that year. However, many men are still affected by unemployment and the growth in jobs has been unevenly distributed: whereas the number of male employees grew by 7 per cent in

London in 1997, it grew by only one per cent in the north and actually diminished in Scotland. Self-employment – which has in the past attracted far more unemployed men than unemployed women – has steadily declined (Convery, 1998e).

Britain's record of male unemployment compares unfavourably with that of other western nations (Table 27, see p49). The report, Employment in Europe 1996 (EC, 1996), described as *'very disturbing'* the increasing rates of withdrawal from the European labour market of men in the prime age group 25-49. It also expressed concern about the continuing trend towards early retirement among men over 50. The report presents comparative data from the different western countries showing that the UK has one of the worst records of male unemployment across all age groups: *'Overall, the largest falls in participation of men of prime working age between 1990 and 1995 occurred in Italy, where it was particularly concentrated in the younger age groups, Denmark, where it was most pronounced for those in the older age groups, Ireland and the UK, where it was relatively uniform across age groups'* (EC, 1996: 48).

The number of men not working because of disability is also markedly higher in the UK than elsewhere: in the European survey 65 per cent of all non-working British men and a massive 74 per cent of those aged 45-49 reported that they were economically inactive for this reason. This may be partly attributable to changes in the method of providing income support and the shift of unemployed people from the unemployment register onto other benefits: *'While there is no evidence that the population is getting healthier, it is thought that much of the reported increase in sickness and disability is due to changing response patterns rather than genuine changes to the health of the population'* (Bell, Houston and Heyes, 1997).

It is well established that the longer unemployment continues, the lower the likelihood of finding a job. Analyses of the destinations of people who participate in government training programmes has shown that the most significant difference relates to the duration of unemployment: those least likely to obtain a job after completion are individuals with the longest record of unemployment. In 1995-96, over half of the trainees who had been unemployed for less than six months before joining Training for Work had obtained a job six months after leaving the programme. Only a quarter of those who had been unemployed for two or more years before joining the programme had obtained a job six months after completing it (DfEE, 1997b).

Geographical variations in unemployment

Long-term unemployment is concentrated within particular localities and communities. The largest proportion of workless households are concentrated in Scotland, Wales, London and the north. Between 1981 and 1991, Glasgow and Manchester lost 30 per cent of blue collar jobs and Liverpool 40 per cent. According to estimates by Sheffield Hallam University, *'real'* unemployment in these cities in January 1997 was 30.6 per cent, 28.6 per cent and 32 per cent respectively (Webster, 1997b).

The most vulnerable male groups

Research by the Institute for Employment Studies (1997) has shown that *'unemployment is not like catching a cold: the risks are far from evenly distributed'.* Some groups are particularly disadvantaged in the job market, especially those with poor literacy and numeracy skills, young people who leave school without qualifications, older workers, black male groups and the homeless.

European data shows that across the European Union a significantly higher proportion of those with low education levels lose their jobs than those with higher skills, irrespective of whether they work in growing or declining sectors (EC, 1996). This trend can be seen in Britain where unemployment levels have risen considerably faster among those with no or lower levels of qualifications than for those with qualifications above A level. For men without qualifications, economic inactivity rates have increased by 12 percentage points in recent years compared with three percentage points for men with qualifications (Bell, Houston and Heyes, 1997). Table 28 (see p49) illustrates how employment status varies according to different qualification levels. In 1997, economic activity rates were 90 per cent among those with higher education qualifications; 79 per cent among those with two or more A levels or equivalent vocational qualifications; 80 per cent among those with five or more GCSE grades A to C (and equivalent) and 60 per cent among those with no qualifications. Workers in the manual occupation groups are far more likely to be made redundant than those in non-manual professions. Eighty-five per cent of those aged over 25 who have been unemployed for over two years are male and nearly 40 per cent have no qualifications (Convery, 1998a).

Unqualified young men

Unqualified young people aged between 16 and 24 are particularly vulnerable to unemployment (Table 29, see p50). Senior associates of the London School of Economics Centre for Economic Performance have claimed that young people are the most marginalised workers in the economy – the last in and first out of jobs. They warn that the situation is worse in the UK than in other OECD states, especially for young men. Across the OECD as a whole, a one per cent rise in overall unemployment leads to a larger rise of 1.13 per cent in unemployment for young people. However: *'The effect is even more marked in the UK where every 1 per cent rise in total unemployment leads to a 1.8 per cent drop in jobs for young people and a huge 2.4 per cent fall for young men'* (Barnard, 1997b).

Between December 1996 and February 1997 there were about 149,000 unemployed 16-17 year olds, only 15 per cent of whom were receiving any form of state income (Chatrik and Convery 1997). Many of these have subsequently become long-term unemployed. In April 1997, over 40 per cent of jobless 18-24 year olds had been unemployed for at least six months – twice as high as the national average. Seventy per cent of these were male and 50 per cent had not achieved level 2 qualifications. Nearly 50 per cent lived in just 10 cities (New Deal Secretariat, 1997).

Ethnic minority men

Analysis of census data (Karn, 1996) indicated that, in the transition from education to work, young people in all minority groups were more likely than whites to experience unemployment when they left school or further education. Far fewer members of black Caribbean, Pakistani and Indian groups than whites obtained full-time employment by the age of 19. In areas such as London, the unemployment rate for 16-24 year-old black males is over 60 per cent.

Unemployment among minority ethnic people in general rose by 2 per cent between 1985 and 1995. In 1996, unemployment rates for black African (28 per cent) and Pakistani men (27 per cent) were three times as high as those for white men (Tables 30 and 31, see pp50-51). Some consider that these figures do not accurately portray the size of the problem. Using data from the Black Employment Institute and Labour Force Surveys, Shire (1997) calculated that in winter 1995-96, the real unemployment rate for black people was 30 per cent and for those aged 16-17, around 55 per cent. This inequality continues throughout adult life. Fifty-three per cent of black people not yet retired are in employment compared with seventy-three per cent of their white counterparts.

The analysis of 1991 census data (Karn, 1996) suggested that the position of black Caribbean men is partly related to their concentration in unskilled occupations. The data showed that only 17 per cent of black men and 13 per cent of black women were in managerial and professional positions, compared with 30 per cent and 20 per cent of white men and women. In spring 1996, 42 per cent of minority ethnic groups worked in non-manual jobs compared with 51 per cent of the white population. The occupations with the highest proportions of minority ethnic workers are plant and machine operatives. Minority ethnic groups are also well represented in some professional occupations reflecting the fact that many immigrants are highly qualified. But inequality persists even for those who are educated and trained. Far more white trainees (64 per cent) have obtained employment after Youth Training than those of Asian origin (39 per cent) or African-Caribbean origin (40 per cent), although similar numbers gain a whole or part qualification. Similarly, the proportion of Training for Work leavers gaining jobs has been lower among those from minority ethnic groups, although there are variations between groups. (DfEE, 1997b). An investigation conducted by the Commission for Racial Equality in the north of England and Scotland in 1996, revealed that although the qualifications of young school and college leavers from minority ethnic groups were similar in all respects to those of white applicants, white people's chances of getting an interview were nearly three times greater than those of Asian applicants and almost five times more than those of black applicants. This led to the conclusion that 'racial discrimination continues to influence the recruitment of young people for work' (CRE, 1997).

Older men

In common with other industrialised societies, Britain has experienced a steady decline in the employment of older men. According to Trinder and Worsley (1997) much of the workforce reduction during the 1980s and 1990s was achieved by early retirement and redundancy for older workers. The economic activity rate for men aged 55-59 has fallen sharply since 1971 and this is expected to continue into the foreseeable future despite the fact that the population is ageing. An OECD report cites Britain as having one of the worst records for expensive early retirement schemes, noting that the most common retirement age for white collar workers is now 57 (Nash, 1998). The economic activity rates of the over 50s are *'markedly lower'* than those aged under 50 (Tillsey, 1995). In spring 1995, 60 per cent of International Labour Organisation (ILO)[1] unemployed men aged 50-64 had been unemployed for a year or more compared with 45 per cent of those aged 20-29 (Social Trends 26, 1996).

The loss of men aged 55 to 59 from the labour market has been a common occurrence in many European Union countries. Although the official retirement age is 65 in most member states and there have been some initiatives aimed at encouraging older workers to remain in or re-enter the labour force, economic activity rates among men over 50 remain significantly lower than those of younger age cohorts: *'There is little sign of the decline in the participation of men aged 50 and over slowing down, despite the shift in policy emphasis in most Member States in recent years away from encouraging early retirement to free up jobs for younger people towards either a neutral stance or one of active discouragement'* (EC, 1996: 49).

The European report suggests that the departure of older men from the labour force is due more to the loss of employment opportunities for this age group than to a preference for early retirement. There also appears to be a strong correlation between this trend and low levels of educational attainment. The European survey found that 57 per cent of men who had withdrawn from the labour force before the age of 60 had a low level of education compared with 43 per cent of those in employment. Under 10 per cent had a university degree or equivalent compared with over 20 per cent of those in work.

1 The International Labour Organisation definition of unemployed is those without a job and available to start work within two weeks following their labour force survey interview and who had either looked for work in the four weeks prior to interview or were waiting to start a job already obtained.

The impact of unemployment

Personal costs

Although unemployment represents a sad waste of individual potential, it affects far more than the psychological, material and financial well-being of the individuals concerned. As well as providing an income, work provides a valuable sense of purpose and status in society: *'Even for those whose wages and conditions are poor, the rhythm of work gives life meaning , the achievement of new tasks, the acquisition of skills and the social intercourse that is part and parcel of the work experience (…) [are] something human beings (…) want and need. Above all, work offers a sense of place in a hierarchy of social relations, both within the organisation and beyond it (…) Those who work belong; those who do not are excluded'* (Hutton, 1996: 100).

It follows that the loss of a job entails multiple loss, not only of money, but of identity, social status, self-esteem and comradeship. The powerful work ethic which persists in western society (even though it is accepted that there will probably never again be full employment) allied to men's attachment to their traditional breadwinner role, inevitably leads to unemployment or cessation of work being viewed as a personal failure. Loss of employment therefore frequently leads to an identity crisis. This applies at different ages. Young men who have never had a job are denied the normal route to adult status while older men who lose or leave their jobs often suffer a process akin to bereavement. It has been found that women adapt more easily to loss of or retirement from paid work and tend to react more positively than men, even though their financial situation is often less secure. While many men strive to preserve their former life style, women develop new activities, often with a view to increasing social interaction: *'In the northern countries, women continue to be defined by what they do while men are defined by what they once were'* (EC, 1997: 8-9).

Employment, in British culture, is so bound up with the male role and identity that its removal or unattainability has a hugely detrimental effect that is still not generally accepted or understood by those who have not suffered from it: *'for many men the experience of job redundancy and unemployment is (…) totally undermining of their sense of masculinity.'* (Kennedy, 1997: 8). The list of negative consequences are well catalogued: feelings of exclusion, despair, loss of confidence and self-respect, alcoholism, domestic violence, family break-up and divorce (Britain has the worst record in the EU).

Social costs

> *'One in four of the country's males of working age is now either officially unemployed or idle with incalculable consequences for our well-being and social cohesion'*. (Hutton, 1996: 1)

Unemployment incurs high costs not only for individuals but also for their immediate family and associates and, ultimately, wider society. It increases family break-up and creates single parent families. Webster (1997a) found evidence in the 1991 census data of an *'astonishingly high'* correlation between lone parenthood and male unemployment which is not taken into account in policies on lone parents. He found that between 1981 and 1991, districts with male unemployment under 5 per cent had an average increase in lone parenthood of less than 3 per cent, whereas districts with male unemployment of over 20 per cent had an average increase of almost 11 per cent (Table 32, see p51). In one part of Merseyside, for example, male unemployment was 27 per cent and the incidence of lone parenthood 23.4 per cent. By contrast in the *'more prosperous'* suburbs of Aberdeen where male unemployment was below 3 per cent, single parenthood was under 5 per cent. Webster extrapolated from this data that an increase of 10 per cent in the male unemployment rate produces a further 8.5 per cent in lone parents as a proportion of households with children.

Male unemployment can affect social stability in other ways. The fact that women are entering the labour force as many men are leaving it, generates a sense of resentment among some men that can lead to domestic difficulties as well as harassment in the workplace: *'More and more men feel as though they haven't made the grade – they feel damaged, injured, powerless, and in need of demonstrating their masculinity all over again. Just when men's economic breadwinner status is threatened, women have come into the workplace in unprecedented numbers as easy targets for men's anger'* (Kimmel, 1997: 48).

There is also an established link between unemployment and crime, particularly among young men. In England, over 60 per cent of offenders nationally are unemployed. In some London boroughs unemployment among young offenders is 80 per cent.

The authors of the report, *Employment in Europe 1996*, single out the UK as the member state where there has been the most marked *'widening in wage disparities between those at the top and those at the bottom of the earnings scale over the past 20 years'* (EC, 1996: 43). They warn that this may create a situation similar to that which has occurred in the US where the loss of men of prime working age from the labour market has also mainly affected low-skilled men and those from minority ethnic groups. The widening gap in earnings between those with low and high skill levels has made it increasingly difficult for these groups to earn an adequate income from legitimate employment. As a result, many men have withdrawn from the official economy and are seeking other ways of earning money, including crime.

Health costs

There is evidence that unemployment also has a negative impact on male health and life expectancy. *'In a society which has not yet accepted that breadmaker can be as valid a male role as breadwinner, evidence continues to accumulate showing that lack of a job destroys masculine self-esteem and undermines health'* (Stepney, 1996). This is exacerbated by the fact that it is linked to diminution of marriage prospects among young men and to family break-up among older ones. Both unemployment and not living with a partner have been found to increase ill health and suicide risk among men (Blaxter, 1990).

Lunneborg (1997) presents data showing that the biggest gaps between the death rates of women and men are at transitional work ages – between the ages of 15 and 30, and between 55 and 70. Moreover, while suicide rates have been steadily decreasing since the mid-seventies for women, they have been rising for men – especially young men. Among those aged 15-19, suicide rates increased by 45 per cent in the decade leading up to the end of the 1980s. Lower skilled men also have a higher suicide rate than others in the population. Four times more men than women commit suicide in UK every year, and according to the Office of National Statistics, unskilled men of working age are more than twice as likely as other men to kill themselves (Utley, 1998).

Despite having a higher mortality rate and experiencing more serious illnesses than women, men are less concerned with their health and less likely than women to consult a general practitioner. They are also likely to confuse physical fitness with good health (Lloyd, 1996; Lunneborg, 1997). For men in the lowest socio-economic groups, life expectancy has actually decreased slightly over the last decade. Studies on the effect of social class on health show that men at the bottom of the social scale live, on average, seven years less than men from the highest social class (Ochert, 1998).

Economic costs

The individual and social costs of low male achievement and associated unemployment are therefore very high. The economic costs are also high. The cost of poor basic skills to UK industry is estimated at more than £4.8 billion per year, about £165,000 for every company employing more than 50 people (Maguire, 1997).

Excluding pupils from school can prove more expensive than providing adequate support for them within mainstream education. Offending behaviour by young men who truant or drop out of the school system also proves costly. Lloyd and Wood (1996) quote estimates from Coopers and Lybrand that crimes committed by young people aged 10-20 cost the country more than £7 billion a year. In 1992, this age group accounted for half of all crimes, the cost of which included: £444 million for criminal damage; £170 million for motoring offences; £160 million for damage during burglary; £582 million for violence against people; £3.5 million for the criminal justice system and £640 million for private security.

Additionally, if individuals are neither learning nor earning, they are not paying taxes, and require social benefits for themselves and their families: *'With each unemployed or non-employed man costing £9,000 a year in lost tax and income support, the transformation in the male labour market is costing the Exchequer over £36 billion a year'* (Hutton, 1996: 185).

• • •

The negative results of male under-achievement are therefore wide-ranging. They are compounded by other social and cultural factors.

Changing gender roles

At a time when men's traditional breadwinner role is being eroded, women's economic position has improved so that they need no longer be financially dependent on a male partner. Although many men have adjusted to this shift, others feel confused, resentful and threatened. They react to changes in the workplace and the perceived advances of women (albeit nowhere near as great as popularly believed) in ways which have been perceptively described as *'fright, flight and fight'* (Woltring, 1996: 761). This can be detrimental to their general health and well-being.

Changing working conditions

Many men who are in employment now work long hours to compensate for the results of organisational *'downsizing'* and increased job insecurity. This has been described as *'presenteesim'* – a long hours culture that particularly affects men (Lunneborg, 1997). British workers work longer hours than their counterparts in the rest of the EU and this can lead to stress and ill health. Lunneborg (1997) quotes a Harris survey which found that British workers suffer more stress-related illnesses than workers elsewhere in Europe. She also quotes a doctor who has noticed increasing levels of stress in the past few years among his male patients.

• • •

There are, then, a number of reasons why we should pay more attention to the problems some men are experiencing particularly as a result of changes in the nature and availability of paid work: *'It is men's changing connection to work – and the sense of identity it confers – that lies behind many of the other key developments affecting their lives, particularly in parenting, health and personal relationships. Although it has become commonplace to acknowledge the general effect of the decline of traditional industries and the rise of mass unemployment on communities, little has been said about the impact on men specifically. Even for men in white-collar jobs, the rapidly approaching end of "the job for life"; even of the very idea of "a career"; together with women's increasing participation in the labour force, is effectively terminating any sense men might have of themselves as "providers". While it is easy to applaud the demise of male domination of the workplace – an outcome certainly long overdue – it is nevertheless still crucial to acknowledge the profound effect such a change has on men's sense of themselves. It cannot be right that so many men are simply left feeling confused, angry, dispossessed and powerless without that experience being publicly acknowledged and discussed'* (Baker, 1996, 32).

There is always a risk of generalisation when dealing with a whole sex and one cannot discount the diversity that exists among individuals. There are some, even in the most disadvantaged groups, who have the temperament, skills and personal resources to survive changes in the labour market and remain in paid work despite few or no qualifications. It would also be simplistic to suggest that all men are suffering and all women are prospering. Men are not society's new victims as some of the more extreme and hysterical claims from men's groups here and in the US would have us believe. Despite significant gains in the labour market, women still experience major disadvantages. Many professions and occupations are still strongly male-dominated as are most decision-making bodies and highest status positions. National Child Development Study data show that men also still earn significantly more than women even if they have similar qualifications (Blundell *et al*, 1997). Thus although many men are disadvantaged in society: *'on the whole women tend to be disadvantage to a far greater extent'* (Pringle, 1996: 222-223). However, acknowledging the inequalities that persist between men and women does not mean we should disregard the inequalities that exist between men and men. As suggested by Ros Coward in a BBC Analysis programme: *'We can acknowledge the alienation and hardship experienced by certain groups of men and areas of male vulnerability without sliding into apocalyptic scenarios about social disintegration'* (Coward, 1998).

The role of education

The question this raises is what role education might have in changing matters. Will increasing male participation in education and training make any difference to those who are most disadvantaged? What can we do? The short answer is a great deal more than we are doing. It is not just a matter of equity and social justice. As a nation we cannot afford either socially or economically to have a large pool of under-educated, under-qualified and under-occupied men.

International comparisons indicate that Britain has a greater problem with inadequate skills than other industrialised countries and lags far behind other European countries in general standards of literacy (Steedman, 1998). Bewick (1997b) refers to the *'long-tail of under-achievement within both schools and the workforce.'* From a purely economic point of view, therefore, greater investment in the education and training of young men could benefit the economy. It could also reduce the costs of judicial processes and custodial care.

Similarly, investing in the training and retraining of unemployed and older male workers (which would mean eliminating the blight of ageism in the labour market) could reduce health, welfare and social expenditure. The report, *Employment in Europe 1996* (EC, 1996), comments on the fact that training and retraining is organised more for young people than for those already in the workplace and older workers who have lost their jobs. It stresses the importance of retraining employees to adapt to new labour market requirements and upgrading and broadening the skills of lower skilled workers to increase their attractiveness to employers and prevent long-term unemployment. In Britain, however, all the evidence points to a persisting failure by employers to train lower skilled and older workers.

Although there are nearly seven million employees without a level 2 qualification, there are still no legislative measures to persuade employers to train all their workers. Moreover, some of the lifetime national education and training targets may have to be adjusted downwards. In 1997, the National Advisory Council for Education and Training Targets (NACETT) published figures showing that the rate of progress towards all of the targets was so slow that there was little likelihood of Britain meeting any of them. NACETT argued that although the British population is better qualified than 10 years ago, urgent action is needed if the targets are to be met by the year 2000: *'The majority of people who will be working in the UK in 2020 are in the workforce now. We cannot rely solely on an influx of highly skilled young people entering the labour market to create a prosperous local and national economy'* (NACETT 1997b: 18).

It would be naïve to expect education or training to overcome all the problems of the most under-qualified groups. However, it has been argued by the co-director of the Centre for the Analysis of Social Exclusion at the London School of Economics that carefully thought-out interventions targeted at low performers could eventually make a difference. He suggests that although education and training may not transform the UK economy as a whole or significantly reduce poverty, skill levels are important and could do much to modify the distribution of earnings at the very bottom: *'If the general skill levels of the lowest qualified were raised it could reduce the supply of low skilled people competing for the supply of jobs. This would tend to raise the wages of the unskilled and improve the prospects of those who have gained the extra skills. In the absence of such a strategy, boosting the supply of low skilled people on the labour market through Welfare to Work incentives will only drive down wages at the lower end even more'* (Glennerster, 1998).

Data from the National Child Development Study (Dearden *et al*, 1997) suggest that work-related training, particularly employer-provided training leading to qualifications, brings rewards in terms of future earnings and employment prospects. A similar claim is made by Karn (1996) in relation to minority ethnic groups. She suggests that there is some point in improving qualification levels even if people do not obtain employment commensurate with them. Young people with qualifications will still get better jobs and have lower chances of unemployment than those with no qualifications. In the long-term, the gaining of qualifications is likely to have a positive effect on employment status, housing and standard of living.

However, it is not just a matter of improving qualifications, employability and skill levels. Education may have much to offer some of the individuals who have profited least from it in the past. Engaging in organised or self-directed learning activities not only imparts new knowledge and skills, it can significantly raise levels of confidence and self-esteem as well as increase feelings of well-being. This can have a positive knock-on effect within families and communities. Raising participation levels among male groups could therefore be in the interests of the wider community and society as a whole. In order to achieve this, however, one needs to understand male attitudes to learning and the reasons why some male cohorts are less motivated to engage in learning than others.

Table 17. GCSE results, England, 1983/84-1995/96

	Percentage of 15 year old pupils achieving:			
	5 or more grades A*-C		5 or more grades A*-G	
	Boys	Girls	Boys	Girls
1983/84	26.3	27.2	71.8	76.6
1988/89	29.8	35.8	76.5	82.2
1989/90	30.8	38.4	77.0	83.7
1990/91	33.3	40.3	80.3	85.8
1991/92	34.1	42.7	79.4	85.3
1992/93	36.8	45.8	81.8	86.9
1993/94	39.1	47.8	83.5	87.9
1994/95	39.0	48.1	83.4	88.1
1995/96	39.8	49.3	83.8	88.2

Sources: Figures for 1983/84 are taken from the School Leavers Survey and are based on school leavers of any age. Figures for 1988/89 to 1990/91 are taken from the Schools Examinations Survey and are based on 15 year old pupils in all schools (excluding special schools). Figures from 1991/92 onwards are taken from the database of School Performance and are based on 15 year olds in all schools

Table 18. School examination results, 1995/96

Thousands

Subject	England GCSE Grades A*-C		Scotland SCE Standard Grades 1-3		Wales GCSE Grades A*-C	
	Females	Males	Females	Males	Females	Males
English	172.9	126.8	24.2	19.8	13.9	10.1
Mathematics	122.7	125.6	16.2	16.0	7.8	7.4
Single Award Science	7.2	4.7	1.9	2.7	0.2	0.1
Double Award Science[1]	106.9	104.5	----	----	3.1	3.1
Biology	13.4	19.5	12.5	5.0	0.8	1.0
Chemistry	12.5	19.8	10.7	10.4	0.6	0.9
Physics	11.5	20.1	6.4	12.4	0.7	1.1
Design and Technology[2]	39.9	30.8	1.4	4.9	4.7	4.1
Home Economics	30.9	3.0	3.7	0.4	2.4	0.1
French	92.2	61.4	13.1	8.4	4.3	2.3
History	64.1	54.3	7.2	4.9	3.1	2.2
Computer Studies[3]	2.6	2.5	3.9	6.3	----	----
	GCE A Level Grades A-E		SCE Higher Grades A-C		GCSE A Level Grades A-E	
English	50.0	21.7	13.6	9.7	2.2	0.7
Mathematics	17.7	31.2	6.6	7.1	0.5	0.7
Bology	23.6	15.8	5.5	2.4	0.5	0.4
Chemistry	13.8	17.4	4.2	4.4	0.5	0.6
Physics	5.4	19.9	2.8	5.6	0.2	0.5
French	14.5	6.6	2.8	0.9	1.3	0.3
History	17.8	14.8	3.2	2.1	1.1	0.8
Computer Studies[4]	1.8	6.9	0.7	2.0	0.2	0.6

Source: Department for Education and Employment, Scottish Examination Board, Welsh Joint Education Committee

[1] Not available in Scotland
[2] Craft & Design in Scotland
[3] Not available in Wales
[4] Technology in England

Table 19. Link between poverty and GCSE results

Free school meals take up and GCSE results: 1995

% of pupils	No. of schools	% A–C	% 5A–G
0–10	987	58	95
11–20	894	42	90
21–30	453	31	84
31–40	231	25	79
41–50	169	22	76
51–60	98	20	73
over 60	74	18	70

Source: OFSTED

Table 20. Achievement rates (%) by mode, sex and by age group, 1994-95

| Age group | Full-time | | | | Part-time | | | |
| | Female | | Male | | Female | | Male | |
	Fully achieved	Partially achieved	Fully achieved	Partially achieved	Fully achieved	Partially achieved	Fully achieved	Partially achieved
16	49	26	46	25	57	9	57	9
17	60	25	56	25	58	11	57	12
18	61	22	56	22	57	10	58	13
19	62	19	58	19	57	9	59	12
20-24	62	17	58	16	60	8	62	8
25+	61	17	56	16	64	8	66	6
All	**59**	**22**	**54**	**21**	**63**	**8**	**64**	**7**

Source: Individualised student record (ISR) 1994-95.
Coverage: 369 colleges, council-funded provision only.
Achievement rates are calculated as a percentage of final year students who have completed their qualifications.
Fully achieved: the student has achieved all of her/his completed qualifications.
Partially achieved: the student has achieved at least half her/his completed qualifications or has achieved at least half the credits or modules towards her/his final qualification.

Table 21. GCE A Level entries and achievements of all candidates in all schools and FE colleges by subject groups and grade, 1994/95, England

Subject Group	TOTAL Men			TOTAL Women		
	Number of entries	Achieved grades A-E	Pass rate	Number of entries	Achieved grades A-E	Pass rate
Sciences						
Home Economics	119	86	72.3	2,230	1,876	84.1
Biological Sciences	18,773	14,240	75.9	28,516	22,223	77.9
Chemistry	21,443	17,370	81.0	16,429	13,421	81.7
Other Science	3,614	2,766	76.5	2,747	2,230	81.2
Mathematics	38,165	32,223	84.4	20.442	17,852	87.3
Physics	24,445	20,374	83.3	6,701	5,629	84.0
Craft, Design & Technology	8,334	7,071	84.8	1,922	1,679	87.4
Computer Studies	7,280	5,470	75.1	1,389	937	67.5
Total	**122,173**	**99,600**	**81.5**	**80,376**	**65,847**	**81.9**
Social Sciences						
Social Studies	24,762	16,692	67.4	48,754	34,737	71.2
History	17,709	14,860	83.9	21,695	17,928	82.6
Vocational Studies	3,167	1,886	59.6	3,187	2,042	64.1
Business Studies	13,706	11,020	80.4	12,054	9,314	77.3
Geography	21,346	17,115	80.2	17,331	14,284	82.4
Physical Education	4,737	4,241	89.5	2,939	2,594	88.3
Economics	15,856	12,384	78.1	8,087	6,057	74.9
Total	**101,283**	**78,198**	**77.2**	**114,047**	**86,956**	**76.2**
Arts						
Religious Studies	1,744	1,530	87.7	5,164	4,537	87.9
Spanish	1,274	1,137	89.2	2,945	2,547	86.5
French	7,493	6,527	87.1	16,967	14,794	87.2
English	24,559	21,248	86.5	55,468	49,103	88.5
German	3,197	2,832	88.6	6,630	5,803	87.5
Communication Studies	7,598	6,015	79.2	13,287	11,334	85.3
Music	2,019	1,816	89.9	3,280	3,042	92.7
Art & Design	12,342	10,709	86.8	18,953	17,292	91.2
Classical Studies	3,063	2,709	88.4	4,097	3,738	91.2
Other Modern Languages	1,807	1,563	86.5	2,415	2,166	89.7
Total	**65,096**	**56,086**	**86.2**	**129,206**	**114,356**	**88.5**
General Studies	28,520	24,265	85.1	28,230	22,242	78.8
All Subjects	**317,082**	**258,149**	**81.4**	**351,859**	**289,401**	**82.2**

Source: Statistics of Education – Public examinations GCSE and GCE in England, 1995. Data refer to candidates of all ages

Table 22. Examination results of students obtaining First Degree qualifications by gender and mode of study, United Kingdom HEIs, 1995/96[1]

Thousands

	Men			Women		
	Full-time	Part-time	Total	Full-time	Part-time	Total
1st	8.8	0.6	9.4	7.3	0.7	7.9
Upper 2nd	42.3	2.7	45.0	54.6	3.6	58.1
Lower 2nd	41.7	2.8	44.4	41.9	3.0	44.9
Undivided 2nd	0.1	---	0.1	0.1	0.0	0.1
3rd	8.1	0.7	8.7	4.4	0.5	4.9
Pass	10.6	4.9	15.6	7.8	5.2	13.1
Total	111.5	11.8	123.3	116.0	13.0	129.0
% 1st and Upper 2nd	46	29	44	53	33	51

Source: HESA Press Release PR12

Table 23. YT leaver outcomes, October 1995-September 1996

	In a job	Gained a Qualification	Completed
White	64%	51%	52%
African/Caribbean	49%	45%	45%
Indian/Pakistani/ Bangladeshi	39%	48%	47%

Source: YT follow-up survey as quoted in Statistical Bulletin, DfEE, May 1997

Table 24. Training for Work – destinations and qualifications by characteristics

England and Wales   Per cent

Period of survey	Period of leaving	Outcome[1]	All Leavers	Gender		Ethnicity				Special Needs Groups		
				Male	Female	White	Black/ African/ Caribbean	Indian/ Pakistani/ Bangladeshi/ Sri Lankan	Other	People with disabilities	Literacy/ numeracy need	English/ Welsh/ Gaelic for speakers of other languages
Oct 1993-Sep 1994	1993-94	In a job	36	33	42	37	25	34	25	29	19	24
		Completed	61	60	62	61	60	65	64	58	56	63
		Gained Qual	41	39	46	42	39	36	40	44	38	37
Oct 1994-Sep 1995	1994-95	In a job	38	35	44	38	27	33	30	33	20	25
		Completed	66	66	65	66	65	68	68	64	64	69
		Gained Qual	45	44	47	45	44	39	41	48	43	43
Oct 1995-Sep 1996	1995-96	In a job	39	36	46	40	32	37	32	37	24	29
		Completed	70	70	69	69	71	71	75	67	69	73
		Gained Qual	48	48	47	48	46	42	48	50	46	46
Oct-Dec 1995	Apr-Jun 1995	In a job	39	37	45	40	30	37	30	38	22	29
		Completed	70	70	70	70	70	72	76	68	70	69
		Gained Qual	53	52	55	53	52	47	53	55	51	48
Jan-Mar 1996	Jul-Sep 1995	In a job	38	36	45	39	30	37	31	36	20	25
		Completed	70	70	69	69	72	71	73	67	68	75
		Gained Qual	51	51	51	51	50	44	52	53	49	52
Apr-Jun 1996	Oct-Dec 1995	In a job	41	37	48	41	35	39	33	38	27	32
		Completed	69	70	67	69	71	70	75	66	67	69
		Gained Qual	42	45	38	43	41	37	44	46	41	41
Jul-Sep 1996	Jan-Mar 1996	In a job	39	35	46	40	34	36	36	38	28	29
		Completed	70	70	70	70	72	74	75	68	69	78
		Gained Qual	44	44	44	45	43	39	43	46	45	41
Oct-Dec 1996	Apr-Jun 1996	In a job	42	39	47	42	35	44	34	40	29	32
		Completed	70	71	70	70	74	73	71	68	70	70
		Gained Qual	44	45	43	45	42	38	41	46	43	41

Source: TfW follow-up survey

1 Gained Qual – the proportion gaining any full qualification and/or credit towards one

Table 25. Highest qualification held by sex and age, people of working age, United Kingdom, spring 1997

Per cent

	16-24		25-39		40-59/64[1]	
	Men	Women	Men	Women	Men	Women
Higher Education	10	10	25	23	22	20
2+ A level or equivalent	22	22	14	9	10	5
Trade apprenticeship	5	2	13	4	21	5
5+ GCSE grades A* to C or equivalent	23	28	11	16	6	11
Qualifications at NVQ level 1 and below	20	20	17	27	6	16
Other – level unknown	3	3	8	5	13	11
No qualification	15	14	10	14	21	32
All (thousands = 100 per cent)	3,282	3,125	6,862	6,665	8,517	7,229

Source: Labour Force Survey

[1] The upper age limit is 64 for men and 59 for women

Table 26, Industrial changes, 1971-96

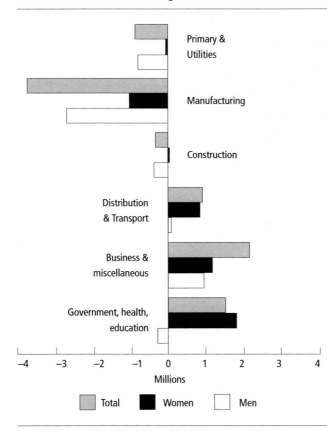

Source: Review of the Economy and Employment (Institute of Employment Research), 1996/97

Table 27. Average unemployment rates (standardised), 1990-97

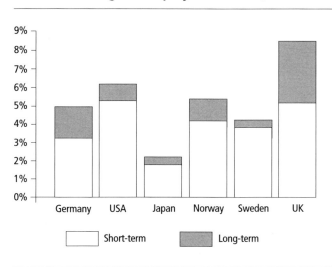

Source: Working Brief, March 1997

Table 28. Economic status, by highest qualification held, people of working age, United Kingdom, spring 1997

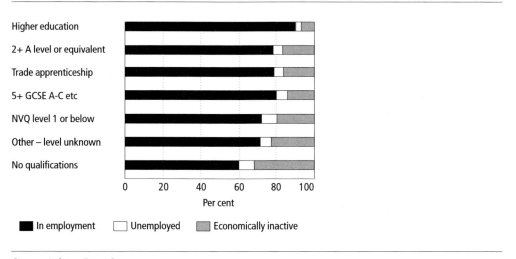

Source: Labour Force Survey

Table 29. Unemployment rate by age group

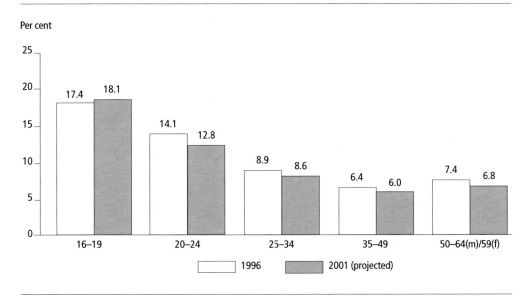

Source: Labour Force Survey, Spring 1996

Table 30. ILO unemployment rate by ethnic origin

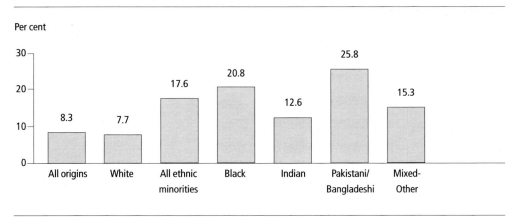

Source: Labour Force Survey, Spring 1996

Table 31. Unemployment rates (LFS) by ethnicity and gender, autumn 1996

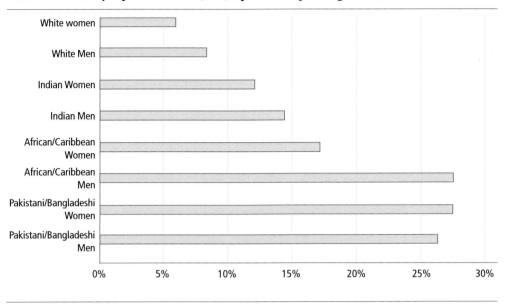

Source: Working Brief, May 1997

Table 32. Increase in women lone parents, 1981-91: GB districts by male unemployment rate

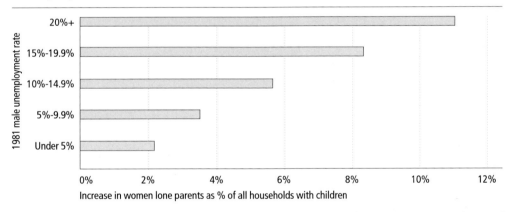

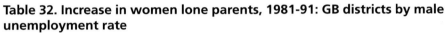

Source: Working Brief, October 1997

CHAPTER THREE

Understanding male attitudes and participation patterns

If we want to change people's attitudes to learning then we need to understand why they have them in the first place. We need specifically to understand why men generally take less advantage than women of the range of education opportunities available. To borrow a phrase used by the Institute of Employment Studies (1997): *'accurate analysis of the causes of disadvantage is crucial to effective policy design'.*

Boys at school

Attitudes to education are formed early and there is already evidence of a gender divide at compulsory schooling age. Surveys have indicated that boys find school more restrictive, less congenial and less relevant than girls who generally have more positive attitudes towards learning and seem more motivated to achieve. Although 16-year-olds attach more importance to improving qualification levels than they did a few years ago, attitude surveys suggest that girls consider it more important than boys who are more concerned with earning money, learning a skill and finding a secure job (DfEE 1997e: 22). This trend was confirmed in a recent research project backed by the Prince's Trust and the DfEE. According to Tyesome (1998), the study found that secondary school girls to be more career-minded than boys and more likely to be planning to stay on in full-time education after the age of 16. Boys were almost twice as likely as girls to be planning to seek a job at age 16. This suggests that boys may be adapting less readily than girls to changing labour market conditions. School studies reviewed by Riddell (1992) also suggest that although girls have changed their expectations to encompass careers as well as family life, many boys still have a stereotypical view of gender roles. There are signs that schools may not be doing enough to encourage more realistic expectations. An HMI report the same year (1992) found that little action was being taken, especially in mixed schools, to counteract gender-stereotyped attitudes and expectations.

More worryingly some teachers have noticed a growing 'anti-education' culture among boys. This appears to be caused by a combination of socio-cultural, economic and educational factors.

Social and cultural factors

Coming from a background where education is neither encouraged nor valued inevitably has a strong influence on attitudes to school. A study of attainment among inner city primary school children showed that a major factor in their success was parental interest and encouragement (Tizzard *et al*, 1998). As observed in Chapter 1, there is also a well established link between social class, educational attainment and positive attitudes towards education that is already apparent at school age.

High male unemployment

Another factor is the changing economic environment and growth of male unemployment. Teachers in areas of high male unemployment have found boys as young as 10 convinced that they will never have a job and therefore already sceptical about the relevance of education. A study of teenage health in Scotland revealed an increase in anxiety and psychological distress among young people. This was attributed to the fear of unemployment and poor family relationships: *'Children were starting to worry about unemployment very early on: one in five 11-year-olds predicted they would be unemployed when they grew up. Young people with a bad relationship with their parents were more likely to drink, smoke, take drugs, did worse at school and had low self-esteem.'* (Ochert, 1998).

Similarly, in a health education project conducted with boys and young men in Northern Ireland, Lloyd found that many were resigned to a life without work (1996).

Awareness of high adult unemployment, particularly if male family members are out of work, can have a detrimental effect on boys' motivations to learn: *'We have to realistically face the new realities of the job market and the changed situation that confronts young men in education. If your dad is unemployed, or only in irregular work, boys can feel in conflict with the predominantly middle-class values of the school, which might think this was a mark of personal failure, and perhaps feel forced to reject the school so that they do not have to feel bad about their fathers.'* (Seidler, 1996: 122).

Lack of positive role models

Many boys have few positive male role models in the home or community and often none who are positively engaged in education. Some argue that childhood has become increasingly 'feminised'. This is particularly the case with boys from African-Caribbean communities, who are allegedly four times more likely than boys from other ethnic backgrounds to belong to single parent families and therefore have even fewer male role models (Sheriffe, 1997). This is compounded by the paucity of male teachers in primary schools. A small research project undertaken in Wales found that both boys and girls performed significantly better in reading ability when they had a teacher of their own sex (Woolford and McDougall, 1998).

There are also few cultural role models to persuade boys of the value of learning. Male sports and pop stars are admired more for their perceived masculine attributes such as physical strength and fitness, risk-taking behaviour and racy life-styles than for their intellect and qualifications.

School curricula and practices

School curricula and assessment procedures may also influence boys' attitudes to learning. There have been a number of changes in schools in recent years and there is a growing view, outlined in Chapter 2, that current teaching, learning and assessment methods suit girls more than boys, as a result of which boys 'switch off', especially from subjects such as English which are seen as soft, feminine areas of the curriculum. Some also fear losing face if they try, but fail, to do well academically: *'It is often easier for boys to drop out, rather than feel that they have failed in front of their friends.'* (Seidler, 1996: 122).

Having just one principal measure of success for the years of secondary schooling – the GCSE which puts more stress on academic than vocational skills – may accentuate some boys' sense of failure. Some argue that greater recognition should be given to different types of learning and that there should be more motivating combinations of academic and vocational study, using modules and units of achievement (Seidler, 1996).

Teacher attitudes

Teacher attitudes have also been cited as a factor contributing to boys' lack of motivation. It is sometimes claimed that teachers are more sympathetic and responsive to girls than boys and there are signs that some have difficulty in dealing with boys from the black communities. The OFSTED report in 1996 found a *'high degree of conflict'* between white teachers and African-Caribbean pupils and concluded that this group, especially boys, had not shared equally in the increasing rate of achievement in schools. In some areas their performance had actually worsened. Sheriffe (1997) claims that this is partly because African-Caribbean boys are automatically perceived by teachers as under-achievers and treated as such.

Problems affecting black pupils

Sheriffe lists several other problems that reinforce under-achievement among black boys: poor socio-economic and home backgrounds; adult lack of understanding of the school system and limited parental, especially paternal – involvement in their education; feelings of being under-valued, and second language difficulties. The interaction of these, according to Sheriffe (1997), lead to many African-Caribbean boys leaving school with few, and in many cases no, qualifications. To mask their frustration, many adopt a US-inspired culture involving a tough demeanour and a specific posture, appearance and language. There is a strong element of peer group influence in this – something which also has a significant influence on boys' attitudes to school.

Peer group pressure

Peer pressure has a major impact on boys' attitudes and behaviour at school both in this country and elsewhere. Studies reviewed by Gallagher (1997: 33-34) relate boys' under-performance in schools to a *'higher level of disciplinary problems than among girls (…) greater propensity to value anti-intellectual and anti-school cultures, and a greater likelihood for peer-group pressure to privilege values other than academic ones'.* Gallagher cites participant observation research in north American schools which found that around the middle years of elementary schooling, at a time when they are shifting their orientation away from adults and towards their peer group, boys begin to change their attitudes towards school. At this stage doing well academically begins to have a stigma attached. Similar processes have been observed in this country: *'A worrying subculture has emerged that is almost anti-education. A lot of it is down to peer pressure being put on boys not to be seen as swots. It has a tremendous impact'.* (Headmaster of a junior school quoted in Chaudhary, 1998).

It is very important for boys to feel accepted by their peers and this means conforming to a set of attitudes and behaviours that are considered appropriately masculine. There is a wide gulf between academic success and 'dominant masculinities' (Seidler, 1996) and being studious does not readily project the image boys try to acquire during adolescence. Those who have academic leanings risk ridicule or bullying from their peers unless they attend a school with a strong study ethos or are good at sport: *'no one makes fun of you if you're working hard in the class as well [as belonging to the football team]'* (O'Sullivan, 1998).

The health education project conducted with boys and young men in Northern Ireland (Lloyd, 1996) revealed that even though many were aware of the importance of school to their future prospects, they were under strong pressure to act in certain 'laddish' ways. This typically involved disruption and mutual ridicule – behaviour which they felt powerless to change.

Developing a masculine identity

Some analysts feel that there should be greater recognition of the kind of stress experienced by boys at secondary school age and the strains they undergo in trying to achieve an acceptable masculine identity: *'The dominant view of masculinity is that a man should be tough, strong, aggressive, independent, rational, intelligent and so on. But the dominant image of children and young people is that they are vulnerable, weak, immature, passive and dependent. This creates a particular contra-diction for boys, which is heightened as adulthood gets nearer, simply because, within the construction of childhood, being a man cannot be achieved.'* (Ruxton, 1996: 82).

According to Seidler (1996: 115-116), masculinity is something that constantly has to be proved and affirmed. This creates a tension for boys, especially at the time of transition to secondary school, as they feel they have constantly to prove and 'police' themselves to ensure that they act in an appropriate male way. This effectively stops them from developing different forms of behaviour: *'they often learn to judge themselves according to a dominant masculinity, even if, at some level, they do not go along with it'.*

Dominant masculinity tends to be the stereotypical kind portrayed by popular culture. As there are few alternative ways of being held out to young men, and no recognised initiation processes or rites of passage through which they can demonstrate their manhood, they are forced to conform to it: *'Masculinity is a public enactment, demonstrated and proved in the public domain before the evaluative eyes of other men. Yet there is no recognisable way in which adolescent men can pass through some ceremony to achieve a secure manhood. As a result, masculinity becomes a relentless test, never completely proved, with always the nagging suspicion that one false move will destroy everything one's done to prove it.'* (Kimmel, 1996: 45).

Although traditional gender stereotypes are still strongly projected in the more popular forms of mass culture (such as the tabloid press, videos and computer games), society itself has changed considerably. There is now a questioning and rejection of 'macho' values and assumptions. This causes confusion for boys at a critical stage of their development. The attempt to adopt a traditional masculine identity in a period when it is no longer universally acceptable, creates a strain which can have a negative affect on their academic progress. Seidler (1996) believes that although they may accept gender equality at an intellectual level, many boys find it difficult to cope with at an emotional level. This is because masculinity has traditionally been constructed as something which is superior to femininity. Thus boys find themselves in a dilemma: either they affirm a traditional masculinity or they accept gender equality which means feeling unsure about themselves as 'real' men. This can lead to considerable inner turmoil and uncertainty for many young men although, outwardly, they feel obliged to present themselves in a way that conforms to a harder notion of masculinity in order to be accepted by their peers. The tension this causes often results in suppression of feeling and avoidance of self-exposure:

> *'Some of the difficulties that boys are having need to be placed historically within a culture that in so many different ways already makes boys feel bad about themselves and on guard against the attacks of others (...) In school, boys often learn to protect themselves through withdrawing emotionally and presenting themselves as cool, detached and uninvolved (...) Feminism has made a great deal of difference to the culture of many classrooms, and boys have often withdrawn, rather than risk sharing feelings or emotions that might be deemed oppressive to girls. Boys find they turn in on themselves and feel 'unsafe' in expressing themselves, for they do not want to 'lose face' in front of their mates. It feels too risky to speak, or at least to speak seriously about oneself. Rather, there is a withdrawal into humour and irony as forms of self-protection.*

> *The ways that boys are feeling about themselves as boys cannot be separated from*

the ways they are learning. For, if boys are taken up at some level with these emotional challenges and feel they have few spaces in which they can explore them, then it will be harder for them to focus upon their learning. They will be more likely to opt out and they might find it harder to express themselves in their learning. They will avoid forms of self-expression that have become so important in contemporary pedagogue, not wanting to expose feelings that might only make them feel worse about themselves. What becomes more important is keeping face in front of your peers and not showing any signs of weakness. Boys then get so used to suppressing what is going on in their inner emotional lives, not wanting to connect to parts of themselves that can leave them feeling exposed and vulnerable to the ridicule of their peers, that they cut off and split from their inner lives and it becomes a habitual pattern that is almost impossible to recognise.' (Seidler, 1996: 117-118).

Kimmel (1996: 47) takes this analysis further, pointing out that anxiety to conform to traditional masculine norms of behaviour leads some boys and men to undesirable extremes in their attitudes and conduct:

'To admit weakness, frailty or fragility is to be seen as a wimp, a sissy, not a real man. This fear of being seen as a sissy haunts men all their lives, but it is never more palpable than during adolescence, that fragile moment of transition between childhood and adulthood, a moment when sexual awakening is coupled with the craving for a secure gender identity. Thus sexuality and gender identity become intimately entwined with one another, and this is the moment when systematically avoiding the feminine becomes crucially important. One's manhood is at stake.

Without clear, definable mechanisms for boys to feel secure in their manhood, we will invent our own, dangerous and destructively-distorted ways to prove it to others, and thereby, hopefully, to ourselves. These efforts are shaped (distorted, really) by those two forces that shape and distort everything else in our culture: sexism and homophobia — the power that men have over women, and the power that some men have over other men. Sexism and homophobia become the organising principles of these distorted initiation processes.'

Not surprisingly, the process of developing a conventional masculine identity affects boys' behaviour at school and their educational performance. A recent study (Power *et al*, 1998) demonstrates its impact on the ways in which *'academic ability is perceived, developed and displayed'*. Drawing on a wide range of research studies, the authors discuss how the attempt to achieve and display an acceptable male image either inhibits achievement at school or encourages and rewards it, depending on social class background and the institutional environment. They cite Willis' (1976) study of working class boys which found that the masculine ideal of manual labour provided this group with a cultural resource that simultaneously compensated for and contributed to, educational failure. Although demand for manual workers has sharply declined since the study was conducted, subsequent research indicates that doing well at school continues to be viewed as a form of feminine behaviour even by boys from different social groups. A study of under-achieving middle class boys, for example, suggested that their poor examination performance could be partly attributed to their view of schoolwork as something effeminate: *[they] located themselves along a continuum of masculinity that ranged from the brutish manliness they associated with manual labour and the essential impotence they saw as characteristic of those whose involvement in mental labour was both committed and industrious.'* (Aggleton, 1987: 73)

Conversely, other studies cited by Power *et al* show that in some learning environments, masculinity is positively associated with academic achievement. This applies mainly to the older (post-16) cohorts. As Epstein (1996) points out, the requirement for boys to display *'a visible and unambiguous'* masculine identity appears to decrease significantly at the sixth form stage. At this point, boys who have successfully negotiated the earlier stages of schooling, start to associate academic success with careers, male status and power: *'Hegemonic masculinity is organised on the macro-scale around social power defined in terms of access to higher education, entry to professions, command of communication and so on and delivered to boys through their formal and informal identification as academic "successes".'* (Connell, 1989: 295)

However, there is a strong social divide between the young men who get to this point and those who retain the values and expectations of the cohorts in Willis' study and drop out of school before or at the age of 16. By this stage, their prospects may have already been damaged beyond repair. Without qualifications, their hopes of finding secure and well paid employment are slim, although they may not see any connection between the two.

Young men without qualifications

The failure to connect educational success with employment carries over into life beyond school. 'Disaffected' young men often fail to see the link between unemployment and educational attainment and in many cases their expectations have not caught up with the changes that have taken place in the world of work. To quote Estelle Morris, former Education Minister, speaking on BBC Radio 4: *'In the past boys didn't have to get examination passes to get a job and their place in society and to get their self-esteem, but that has changed now. One of the problems with boys' underachievement is that they haven't latched onto that.'* (*Analysis.* 5 March, 1998)

Perceptions of irrelevance

The attitudes of young people towards education are inevitably shaped by their view of its relevance and potential benefits. Those who live in areas with high levels of long-term unemployment may not view education or training as a route to jobs. Others may be put off by the apparent irrelevance of education and training to the world of work. One analyst has suggested that the current stress on key skills may deter young men who are already disenchanted with school and want only to learn 'hard', specific work-related skills:

> *'Any shift in the emphasis of further education at entry level to include a greater number of key skills has a price attached. An increase in key skills can only be achieved within a fixed programme template by reducing the time spent on vocationally specific training. This change risks high dropout and failure rates among young people, many of whom are desperate to leave a general education system behind (i.e. one which teaches mathematics and English in an environment devoid of vocational context)…*

> *A high proportion of young people have left school and chosen entry level programmes precisely because of their vocational context and their perceived practical nature. To the learner the focus at all times must clearly remain associated with a career outcome, something they perceive to be tangible. The move to broader, less focused qualifications at this level is likely to prove a hurdle to recruitment for colleges and hence reduce opportunity and access for a significant number of young people…particularly in those areas traditionally regarded as being "practical" or where a strong cultural qualification pathway exists…It's time we rediscovered the nature of skills training and stopped pretending that all learners will thrive on a diet of key skills. How do you sell a GNVQ Landbase course to a young person who wants to be a farmer or forester if it includes a small amount of what they want to do but lots of things they don't want to do, heaps of useful key skills?'* (Atkin, 1997).

Continuing lack of male role models

Some point to the declining number of role models who might attract young men aged 16+ into further education or training. According to a college development worker working with this group the number of male lecturers is declining: *'Young men need men to relate to. Lots of them don't have role models. That's a growing problem. Colleges are getting things on the cheap. That means part-time and that means women.'*

Financial and socio-economic deterrents

For many young people from low income families, finding work is a greater priority than gaining qualifications. In his study of staying-on rates in Northern Ireland, Armstrong (1997) found a strong correlation between parents' economic activity and status, and the participation of young people in education. If parents are unemployed, young people may be motivated to enter the labour market as soon as possible in order to add to household finances. If parents are working, their occupational status has a bearing on their offspring's attitudes to education: *'Young people whose parents are employed particularly in non-manual occupations, have relatively high educational participation rates. This can largely be understood in terms of either an income effect (i.e. there is less pressure on such young people to begin to contribute to household income post-16) or else an attitudinal effect (e.g. the parents of such young people are likely to have stayed on in post compulsory education themselves and so may encourage their offspring to do so). One important implication of these findings is that relatively poor educational standards seem to be transferred, to some extent, between successive generations.'* (Armstrong, 1997: 32).

This confirms DfEE findings for England and Wales referred to earlier in Chapter 1 (Table 4, see p15).

Offending behaviour

Many young men from working class backgrounds who leave school without qualifications subsequently find themselves without work and ineligible for welfare benefits at a vulnerable age. They may lack accommodation, parental support, and finance. As they are outside the structures provided by education or employment, they can be hard to reach by outside agencies. Without employment they miss out on a crucial passage to adulthood and responsibility, and, lacking an income, some resort to crime. It is often the male peer group that reinforces this process as a study for the Audit Commission has found: *'Boys who said they had friends who committed offences were eight times more likely than others to admit to offending. Young people frequently offend in groups of two or three, rather than alone. Having delinquent friends reinforces any predisposition towards crime and makes it more difficult to break out of a pattern of offending behaviour.'* (Audit Commission, 1996: 119).

Ruxton (1996: 82) argues that the wider social processes involved in learning to be a man — the norms acquired through male peer groups in schools, pubs and workplaces and reinforced by advertisers and the media — contribute to male offending behaviour. It is something which, unlike young women, young men do not quickly grow out of, especially if they are in poor economic circumstances: *'The Home Office (1995) self-report study identifies the main factors in young women growing out of crime as leaving home, entering into stable relationships with the opposite sex, forming new families, and eventually becoming economically independent, socially responsible and self-reliant individuals. For young men, none of these factors were found to be statistically associated with giving up crime (…) desistence was more gradual and intermittent, with attempts to stop often thwarted by events or changes in circumstances. The positive effects of personal and social developments tended to be outweighed by the more powerful but largely negative, influences of the peer group.'* (Ruxton, 1996: 84).

The disadvantages faced by young black men

Minority ethnic youths are particularly vulnerable. Many lack the information and support structures that might help them access opportunities and sources of financial help and they may be reluctant to undertake training due to bad experience or expectation of racial discrimination (Chatrik, 1997a). Analysis of 1991 census data (Karn, 1996) showed that being born in this country is not associated with any improvement in life chances. The fact that there is a penalty for all minority ethnic groups, whether first or other generation, strongly suggests an element of discrimination. According to Karn, the lack of progress for second generation members of minority ethnic groups has serious implications: young people, particularly those born in the UK, may be sceptical about the relevance of educational qualifications and their chances of receiving equal treatment in the job market. This is likely to have an effect on their educational participation rates and on the relative attractions of alternative sources of income which do not carry an ethnic penalty, such as theft and drug dealing.

Although African-Caribbean males represent under two percent of the total population they are disproportionately represented in the prison population, accounting for approximately 10 per cent of inmates.

• • •

For a number of reasons, therefore, it is difficult to attract unqualified young men back into education. These reasons are compounded by the fact that young men can be difficult to contact, especially if they are homeless. However, obstacles to their participation are also created by shortcomings in the operations of the agencies and services that work with them. Merton (1997a) lists these as: inappropriate staff attitudes and skills, low levels of coordination between providers and referral agencies, bureaucratic regulations, inflexible funding regimes, unclear information, insensitive guidance procedures and unevenly distributed education and training provision. The Audit Commission (1996: 76) has also commented on the unevenness of services for young people and the frequent neglect of those most in need of support: *'The resources devoted to youth work vary widely between authorities in level and in the way in which they are used. Local authorities are required to provide an "adequate service" for the personal development of young people, through informal social education. This leaves great scope for local interpretation in coverage, target age group, priorities, staffing, facilities and methods of youth services. Most youth workers view their role as providing a universal service to young people and are unwilling to target their efforts on areas of high deprivation or on those at risk of offending.'*

The image of Youth Training Schemes

It is hoped that the New Deal will help many disaffected young people to improve their life chances. Early evidence on the progress of the programme has indicated that, probably for the reasons listed above, most of the young people eligible are more concerned to take up employment than the education or training option. This may also have something to do with the image of previous youth training programmes. Some young men have already been on a series of training schemes, often repeating the same programmes, with no meaningful employment outcomes.

Midgeley (1997b) points out that although completion and attainment rates in youth training have improved substantially in recent years, programmes still suffer from the negative image that evolved after the establishment of the Youth Opportunities Programme (YOPs) in the 1980s. This led to a widespread perception that youth training was a last resort for 'no-hopers' and a punishment for unemployment which, at best, could lead to menial jobs with exploitative employers. This analysis was confirmed in a survey to investigate young people's impressions of youth programmes: *'They were at best sceptical saying that they were unhelpfully short-term, provided insignificant rewards and offered poor quality experiences. Consequently their feelings of isolation and low self-esteem were only intensified.'* (Merton (1997b).

Similar views were expressed by unemployed 16- to 17-year-olds not involved in training during a survey conducted in Mid Glamorgan. None of the individuals interviewed saw any benefit in Youth Training: they were more interested in jobs in the informal labour market than formal labour market jobs and training which were seen to be low paid and restrictive (Maclagan, 1997c). Merton (1997a) argues that young people in this situation consider the financial benefits to be derived from low level vocational qualifications to be too small or too long-term to justify investment in learning.

Despite such findings, minimum hours for trainees on Youth Training and Modern Apprenticeships schemes in England were lowered by almost half in 1997. Moreover some youth training schemes have actually excluded the most needy young people. The Audit Commission (1996: 83) criticised the way in which most of the funding for local Training and Enterprise Councils (TECs) has been allocated: *'according to the number of trainees that they succeed in helping into employment or to gain qualifications, leaving little incentive to train those who are less able – including young offenders and young people with poor educational records. Some special funding is available for schemes to assist those who have been unemployed for long periods of time or who have special needs. But there is little money available, for instance, for training to NVQ level 1.'*

It has also been reported that some employers are recruiting graduates onto Modern Apprenticeships: *'It cannot be fair that graduates are getting this level of support when you have so many other young people unemployed.* (Chatrik, 1997a).

The Government is addressing the problem of low qualification level with the New Deal. However, it may take time for the most under-qualified young men to adjust their perceptions of training and education. The same applies to many male non-participants over the age of 25.

Men over 25

Cultural factors

Some of the gender differences in attitudes to education that are evident among school pupils persist in adulthood. The 1997 National Adult Learning Survey (SCPR, 1997) found men more likely than women to say that nothing would encourage them to learn (a resistance more prevalent among older men); more likely to report employment pressures and more likely to say that they prefer to spend their free time doing other things. They were also more likely than women to say they had not enjoyed learning at school and less likely to be worried about costs or a perceived lack of ability (Table 33, see p74).

As with boys at school, a powerful obstacle to men's involvement in organised education and training – particularly during the prime working years – is the perception of what constitutes appropriate masculine behaviour. This is not to suggest that all men embrace dominant forms and expressions of masculinity, however, many: *'still cannot let go of the old patterns and stereotypes despite the well-recognised negative effects of gender socialisation for men. It would appear that the privilege of being male in a patriarchal society is too much of an enticement.'* (Young, 1996: 217)

The perceived imperative to conform to a 'proper' masculine way of behaving has a marked impact on different life dimensions. Recognising and acting on ill health may be seen as unmanly *'Does Rambo visit his GP or ask for margarine and not butter?'* (Lloyd, 1996: 48)), as may admitting ignorance. Studies also show that men fear exposing educational limitations and deficiencies and are reluctant to express needs or emotion. The suppression of needs can, if taken to extremes, lead to violence, alcohol and drug abuse, untreated illness and suicide (Lunneborg, 1997).

Male conformity can also lead some men to engage in activities they find uncongenial. In a study of men studying for degrees at the Open University, one interviewee described the pressures he experienced in his working life to behave in a typical male way: *'I was expected to join organisations like the Junior Chamber of Commerce. It was more like the boys' club with the undercurrent of chatting each other up for business. They forced you into professional circles, bankers, solicitors, accountants, so they'd invest money in your building society. You were all pally with them, played golf. I never spent my expense account because I didn't enjoy those business lunches. I'm not a guy's guy, I'm not really interested in football, rugby, motor racing, the manly things supposedly.'* (Lunneborg, 1997: 16)

Gendered learning choices

Similar pressures can influence men's attitude to education and choice of study area. Different areas of the curriculum have come to be regarded as essentially masculine and feminine, reflecting the strongly sex-segregated labour market: *'Not only are certain subjects seen as more suitable for men than women, but also (...) these subjects in themselves seem to embody qualities that are linked to ideas about "masculinity" and "femininity". For example, physics is seen as hard and factual and masculine, whilst home economics is seen as practical, caring and feminine. "Knowledge" as a whole becomes compartmentalised, with the result that some kinds of knowledge are considered more important than other kinds and this is communicated very effectively in schools and other institutions.'* (Tett, 1994: 47)

As noted in Chapter 1, men tend to gravitate towards the harder, more vocational subjects, with a stress on work-related knowledge and skills. For some groups, to engage in ostensibly feminine areas of the curriculum would threaten traditional gender roles and their male status. As more women enrol in these areas, they become increasingly feminised. As a result the curriculum, particularly in adult and community education centres, continues to reflect and reinforce traditional gender roles and identities: *'Much of the current provision within community education is of programmes designed along sexually stereotyped lines which emphasise women's roles as mothers and household managers and men's as workers and providers. These messages do not convey emancipatory knowledge and may solidify values and attitudes that cause women and men to accept gender relations rather than question them.'* (Tett, 1994: 47).

Education and work

As men see their primary role as that of worker, the perceived value of education depends on the extent to which it assists them in obtaining and maintaining employment. If they have a relatively secure job that they can perform without difficulty, they may not see the relevance of engaging in education or training. This position emerged in a TEC-funded research project on men and further education in North Yorkshire involving over 1,000 men of different ages. Typical comments from non-participants were:

> *'I don't need to go – I've got all the qualifications I want.'*
> *'I have no reason to go – I have a job and can do it.'*
> *'A lot of men don't need qualifications so they don't bother to go.'*
> *I'm happy sticking with what I know.'*
> (North Yorkshire TEC, 1997).

If, on the other hand, they are unemployed and their experience of education, training or retraining has neither assisted them in keeping a job nor in finding another one, then the value and relevance of education is similarly called into question (McGivney, 1992).

Social class issues

Men's powerful orientation towards employment largely explains why they do not engage in general and non-vocational learning in anything like the same numbers as women. However, there are strong cultural and class factors that lead to variations in attitudes and participation behaviour. Some (mainly middle class) groups see engaging in vocational education and training as a route to career advancement, status and financial rewards; others, especially those who are unemployed or in insecure jobs, see it as a retrogressive step which represents failure to make the (male) grade.

Characteristics such as race, occupational status and social class have a strong impact on attitudes to learning as each is associated with particular cultural pressures and norms. For some groups it is normal to engage in organised learning activities. Non-learners, however, often belong to social groups for whom participating in taught learning is *not* part of normal adult behaviour patterns and to do so could lead to their being perceived as odd or out of step with their associates or the rest of the community. In their study of workplace training, Fuller and Saunders (1990: 9) found an anti-training culture among manual workers in some workplaces *'because to engage in training is tantamount to breaking ranks'*. Those who participate despite this sense of growing solidarity sometimes experience a sense of displacement from their roots and class (O'Shea and Corrigan, 1979).

Working class men

White male manual workers are the most difficult group to attract to organised learning programmes and, according to some practitioners, the group most neglected by educational policy and provision. Although they are the segment of the population that has been most affected by industrial change and economic restructuring, little has happened to encourage and facilitate greater participation by this group in education and training. However their lack of participation is in part due to attitudes and expectations. In some communities there is evidence of persisting, fixed attitudes to gender, education and work. Education continues to be seen as the province of young people and women, while work is seen as the rightful province of men: *'Education is seen as what women do and is acceptable for them. They can leave the labour market without on the whole incurring disapproval. Men can't or feel they can't do this, because of the nature of their role. Male working-class culture values traditional masculine and physical strength, work involving exertion, over books, study etc. which are seen as for the effeminate and work shy. Education is not work.'* (Mac an Ghaill, 1996)

The North Yorkshire study of men and further education showed the extent to which concerns about image and status affect male attitudes to re-entering education (North Yorkshire TEC, 1997). Although local colleges were viewed very positively, particularly by students over the age of 25, the responses as a whole revealed traditional and stereotypical views of gender roles, as illustrated by some comments by interviewees:

> *'College is a step up for women, it's a step down for men.'*
> *'Women are more likely to be supported by men rather that vice versa, so it's easier for those women to go.'*
> *'Going back to college – you'd be embarrassed – like having a Jaguar for twenty years then going on the bus.'*

Inevitably perceptions differed with age. Whereas 16- and 17-year-olds saw attending college as an escape from school, adults saw it as going *back* to school. Regardless of age, however, respondents had similar views of what constitutes appropriate behaviour for men and women at different stages of life. There was a widely held view that men of working age who were attending full-time courses were likely to be doing so out of necessity rather than choice. Respondents also believed that men who participate in education have far more to lose, in terms of status and image, than women. Among participants over the age of 25, one of the most frequently expressed worries was fear of failure and loss of face. Some had experienced negative reactions from employers and colleagues which reinforced the view that it is abnormal for an adult male to be learning rather than earning. The research report sums up their dilemma as follows:

> *'Being a student (as your main occupation) is not seen as a desirable, high status activity for older men. Even those who had made a positive choice to change career and so were attending college to pursue this aim were not viewed in a very positive light: "They should be sorted by that age." (19-24 year old, employed). A further factor was the perceived pressure on men to: "put bread on the table" (35-49 year old, unemployed). Men who were not seen as fulfilling this role of being a "good provider" were seen as running the risk of attracting social disapproval, or worse, pity.*

> *The views expressed by men under 25 at college were that although they did not think that older men should not be at college, they also thought that it could be difficult to be at college if you were older. Older men from all the groups also felt that if a man wished to go (back) to college when he was older then he should be encouraged to do so but that going when you were younger "fits better into a life plan".'* (North Yorkshire TEC, 1997: 16-17).

In his study of Access students, Neville (1996: 55-56) found that some men were in a similar situation: their decision to return to study was viewed by others as inappropriate behaviour for a man: *'The feeling that one is out of synchronisation with age stages can be a propellant towards education but can induce a sense of guilt in some students that they have had to take these steps to sort their lives out. The criticism directed at male students appeared on the whole to be for the apparent pointlessness of their studies. Why were they not "out looking for a job?" The older the student, the sharper this criticism (...) "my friends consider a return to study at my age (30s) is one step above being permanently unemployed".'*

Similar findings were reported several decades ago when, during the run down of major industries such as coal and steel, there were attempts to encourage redundant workers to participate in education and training schemes. Following the closure of the Consett steelworks, for example, only about 30 per cent of the unskilled and semi-skilled workers eligible took advantage of a free education and training programmes arranged for them. Their reluctance was attributed to a combination of anxiety, lack of confidence and a feeling that for men, a return to education would be abnormal and entail loss of face (Further Education Unit, 1985).

The impact of unemployment
Some studies have indicated that instead of motivating men to seek education or training in new skills, the loss of a job leads to scepticism about

the value of training (McGivney, 1992a). People who have been doing unskilled jobs without benefit of training do not see any value in undertaking training. Those who have been trained and have subsequently been made redundant often resist undertaking other, potentially useless, training.

Difficulty in adapting to changing conditions

In areas where traditional industries have disappeared, many unemployed manual workers (and their sons) are still reluctant to consider other kinds of work, even though the manual jobs they want are no longer available. According to the manager of a careers service in Coventry: *'you get lads saying to you I just want a job but the sort of jobs they want no longer exist. It is particularly hard dealing with people who are second or third generation unemployed because their ideas of work are in the past.'* (Edwards, 1997b)

Thus, in working-class communities where male culture is strongly based on manual labour, poor educational attainment and low aspirations can be perpetuated.

Many working-class men are therefore experiencing a cruel dilemma: the kind of employment they want is in short supply but their sense of identity is so bound up with traditional labour that they find it difficult to engage in different jobs or alternative activities. Some are consequently failing to adjust to changed social and economic conditions and their basic assumptions and expectations, especially regarding gender roles, have not caught up with the cultural transformations that have taken place over the last decades. It is this cultural time lag that is affecting the well-being of some men. Some see it as a phenomenon that affects the entire sex. Kimmel (1996: 44), for example, argues that one of the major problems confronting men today is their reluctance to change: *'Our lives have changed dramatically, but what has not changed are the ideas we have about what it means to be a man. The structure of our lives has changed, but not their culture, the ideologies that give that structure meaning. This is what social scientists used to call "culture lag"; where the technology and institutional framework of a society changes more rapidly than the culture's stock of meanings and interpretations of social structure. The 1990s have found men constantly bumping up against the limitations of the traditional definition of what it means to be a man, but without much of a sense of direction about where they might go to look for [an] alternative (...).'*

In some respects, of course, male behaviour has changed – it is much more common than in previous generations for men to shop and look after children, and relationships between the sexes have also evolved. However, there is still: *'a male culture which exists unchanging while everything else has been transformed all around'* (Grant, 1998). This constitutes one of the greatest barriers to male participation in education.

Although cultural and social factors have a strong bearing on male attitudes to education there are also, of course, many practical reasons for men's non-participation.

Competing demands on time

A particular obstacle is lack of time because of other commitments. For men, education has to compete with work and range of other activities and interests. They also spend more time than women on leisure activities. Whereas there are few public places women can comfortably frequent on their own, particularly in the evenings, and education centres and institutions provide a 'safe' environment in which to meet others and engage in activities outside the home, men have access to a wider range of public places such as pubs, clubs and sports centres. The 1996 NIACE/Gallup survey (Sargant *et al*, 1997) showed that by far the most popular leisure interests for men were physical activities such as sports.

Finance

There is evidence that the inability to pay for learning is a huge barrier to many people in low income groups. In the North Yorkshire study, it was a key concern for male participants in both the younger and older cohorts, especially if they were in receipt of state benefits. Sheriffe (1997) has also found that the main external barrier stopping African-Caribbean men from attending college is finance.

Spending on discretionary awards for further education students fell by over 50 per cent between 1992 and 1997 and in some local authorities they have virtually been abolished. Even if courses are free, the costs of transport, books and equipment can prove an insuperable obstacle for students who are not eligible for housing benefit and income support. Although there are some welcome new initiatives such as an increase in Access Funds that will help some people to participate, the lack of financial support for part-time learners still creates an obstacle for many men, especially those with families.

Institutional factors

The image and ethos of education centres and institutions can strongly affect participation patterns. Some are organised more for administrative convenience than for the convenience of learners. No matter how accessible institutions claim or aspire to be, they will not recruit non-traditional learners if their image and 'body language' contradict their words. For example, some higher education institutions, notably the old universities, have done little to indicate that they are not predominantly preoccupied with school leavers, full-time students and people seeking professional status. Those institutions which habitually attract a full complement of students may not be concerned with their social and ethnic composition or even be aware that some segments of the population are habitually missing.

Similarly, some further education institutions have not yet done enough to change their image and broaden their appeal to adults. Because colleges used to focus mainly on the 16-19 cohort some have, albeit unconsciously, retained a culture related to younger learners that is discernible in the language used, the attitudes and assumptions of staff and the facilities (or lack of them) available. These signs are quickly picked up by adults, as emerged in the North Yorkshire study of men's participation in further education. Male respondents to the survey, both participants and non-participants:

> 'shared the view that further education is set up for kids. The college environment, facilities, work and study spaces and, to some extent, the "culture" in terms of staff-student relationships are seen as being geared for the younger age groups. In particular men at college over 25 expressed strong views about the prevailing culture that seemed to dominate some college environments both with regard to teaching styles and concerning the informal uses of private study spaces for students within colleges.' (North Yorkshire TEC, 1997: 17)

There was also a view that colleges could not accommodate working men, especially those working shifts. 'I work full-time on shifts and that would mean that I would miss too many sessions'.

Many of the recommendations arising from this study are substantially the same as those suggested in the NIACE publication *Opening Colleges to Adult Learners* (McGivney, 1992b) over five years ago.

Just as further education is seen as a service for young people, so adult and community education is seen as a service for women and consequently has a limited appeal for men. This is partly because they are staffed mainly by women. In addition, (as Tett (1994) points out) many adult and community education programmes are designed to help women gain new interests and achieve personal goals therefore do not attract men who have a more instrumental attitude to learning. In many areas, the kind of adult education programmes that used to have a majority of male participants – woodwork, car maintenance, DIY – have been cut or reduced in number to save costs.

The informal learning methods employed in adult and community education also appeal more to women than to men: 'Men appear to find methods which draw on their personal experiences unattractive whereas women find the opposite. Community educators rarely use the didactic authoritative methodology which men may find more acceptable and so, when men do take part in education, they are likely to find such provision uncomfortable.' (Tett, 1994: 46)

In adult and community education the problem of male non-participation is self-perpetuating. It is difficult to attract men to community learning schemes such as family learning projects so these attract mainly women. Because of this they end up being seen as exclusively for women and thus become, effectively, feminised.

Attempts to attract men by mounting courses in subjects they are ostensibly interested in, such as IT, sometimes founder. This has been attributed both to the feminine image of community education and to men's reluctance to admit learning needs. In one WEA district, for example, learning software has been developed for supported, computer-based, open learning delivery of an Open College Network accredited, Return to Study programme. The intention was to create a cost-effective and sustainable, flexible mode of learning for adult returners of both sexes. Despite the best efforts of workers, however, neither the conventional programme nor the computer-based, open learning version of it have attracted men. According to the project director:

> 'In the past year I have been approached increasingly by advocates on behalf of men although men themselves have been conspicuous by their absence. Some action research we are collaborating in suggests that the reasons may be the same as those which hold them back from other educational opportunities – i.e. that to admit to needing support with this or any other basic skill (in the broadest sense of the phrase) is tantamount to admitting a "failure", particularly if the provision is recognised as non traditional. I also think it likely that because I worked through community and guidance contacts locally when recruiting, many of whom discriminate positively in favour of women, another approach will be needed if we are to raise its profile locally with men. We have now been approached by a major employer who would like to discuss the possibility of carrying out an external field trial with an all male group of shop-floor employees in the workplace during 1999.'

Structural disincentives

The reluctance of some groups of men to engage in education and training cannot be wholly attributed to lack of interest, fear of failure or the embracing of traditional masculine values. As argued in an earlier study (McGivney, 1992a), it is not always lack of motivation that stops some groups from engaging in education and training: there are a number of structural factors that militate against their participation, not the least of which is sheer lack of opportunity. The evidence suggests that some of the 'missing' men are not deliberately avoiding education: they are systematically excluded from it by employers, education institutions and the system governing programmes and welfare benefits for the unemployed. Policy decisions, funding regimes and provider practices often combine to serve the interests of more affluent and educationally experienced learners, while effectively, though perhaps unintentionally, blocking access to other groups. This interacting process has been described by McIntyre: *'Participation patterns are the result of an interplay of government funding regimes, provider cultures and strategies, the demands of adult learner clienteles and the character of the community being served (...) In the absence of a funding regime which requires equity outcomes, participation is narrowed to clienteles resident in more affluent areas and advantaged in terms of qualification, employment and income. The needs and interests of these clienteles then shape the content and culture of provision. Provision and participants are mutually shaping. This provides one explanation of the participant profiles that are typical of institutionalised adult education.'* (McIntyre, 1998).

The process McIntyre describes has been apparent in the UK for some time. The 1992 Further and Higher Education Act, for example, led to reductions in LEA-provided adult education classes as well as in concessionary fee arrangements. This has disproportionately affected some groups such as older adults. In further education, the curtailing of the demand-led funding element has also negatively affected adult access as have selective admissions procedures. It has been found that some colleges are under pressure from employers to discriminate in the allocation of work placements and sponsorships, as a result of which black men can find it difficult to enrol in training programmes (Karn, 1996).

Unequal access to employer-supported training

A report for the Institute for Fiscal Studies led to the conclusion that *'unequal access to qualifications and training is a major determinant of entrenched inequalities in Britain today'* (Bewick, 1997-98). In a report on progress towards the National Targets for Education and Training NACETT (1997b) points out that about one third of employees (particularly those in small organisations) have not been offered any training by their current employer; that two thirds of organisations with over 50 employees have not gained, or are not committed to, the Investors in People programme and that only 5 per cent of the workforce have a National Vocational Qualification.

Labour market surveys consistently show that most employer-provided training is offered to people in higher level jobs, those with higher qualifications and younger employees. Older and unqualified workers are the groups that invariably miss out. The data show both that employer-provided training diminishes with age and that those with no qualifications receive the least (Tables 34 and 35, see p75). Older workers tend to be less qualified than younger ones. Sixty-seven per cent of people aged 45-60 hold qualifications and 19 per cent, higher qualifications, compared with 87 per cent and 24 per cent respectively in the 35-34 group. However, little action has been taken to increase the qualification levels of older people. In spring 1996, less than 8 per cent of employees between the age of 50 and retirement had received training compared to just under 15 per cent of all employees of working age.

This inevitably affects individual 'employability'. A survey involving interviews with over 11,000 people revealed a clear correlation between unemployment and lack of training opportunities (Dex and McCulloch, 1997). Those who had lost their jobs, both men and women, were less likely to have had any training before becoming unemployed than the average person in the sample. Minority ethnic individuals reported fewer training spells than white people and less employer-funded training, a gap that was particularly large for men: 13 per cent of men from minority ethnic groups reported employer-funded training compared with 42 per cent of white men. The findings also suggested a link between unemployment and *'certain lower level occupations which are to some extent sex-specific such as craft and service, plant and machine and sales occupations'*.

Absence of employer-supported training reinforces non-participation in other forms of learning. Adults whose social and working environments provide few educational opportunities and do little to demonstrate the value and benefits of learning, are unlikely to consider learning as an option for themselves.

Programmes for the unemployed

According to a European report, the UK has *'one of the lowest rates of public spending on training in the European Union'* (European Commission, 1996). Since this critique, there have been even more reductions and changes in employment services. Murray, (1997) reported that during 1996-97, one of the most popular and effective options for unemployed people – Jobclubs – lost 90,000 places and 30 per cent of their budget, while compulsory jobsearch and interview programmes were expanded. Some consider that the elements of compulsion in government programmes bias unskilled men even more against voluntary learning, especially in view of the poor record some programmes have of leading to paid work (Neville, 1998, letter to author).

It is clear that some former training schemes have provided unemployed men with little of real value or relevance and the suspicion remains that they are intended more to keep unemployed figures down than to help people into jobs.

The benefit system

Another structural factor that acts as a strong disincentive to participation in education is the benefit system. As Uden argues (1997), national education and training targets and initiatives tend to have been aimed mainly at those currently employed. Conversely, engaging in learning has not been regarded as a positive outcome from some unemployment programmes. Unemployed people receiving the Job Seeker's Allowance have been dissuaded from learning part-time by restrictions on the courses they can pursue, the length of time they can study and the requirement to leave a course if a suitable job is offered. Research into the effects of the 16-hour study rule by the Unemployment Unit, indicated that unemployed people, although they may have a wish to study, experience a range of problems: inconsistent operation of the rules by different benefit offices and staff members; different definitions of full-time and part-time courses; and disruption of learning programmes because of having to attend compulsory interviews and government programmes. Several colleges responding to the study had found a fundamental incompatibility between students' desire to gain a qualification and the Employment Service's need to meet specified targets: *'although Employment Service staff may understand the value to a claimant in tasking a part-time course they are operating in a difficult climate where they must meet certain performance targets'.* As a result, some jobless people who wish to gain access to learning opportunities are unfairly penalised (Donnelly, 1997).

Although there are plans to relax the 16-hour rule, and less restrictive pilot schemes are already operating in some parts of the country, it may take a while to reassure people that it is now acceptable to participate in education: *'recent reforms have not shifted the underlying pressure that comes from an enforced administrative belief that studying is skiving whereas filling in application forms is a proper use of time paid for by income support.'* (Gardener, 1997).

There are also some unresolved questions about whether the long-term unemployed who come under the New Deal will be permitted to undertake study above NVQ level 2. Although government guidelines suggest that some people undertaking study above this level may be allowed to continue, there are some fears that people may have to leave courses at level 3 if these are not deemed to be leading to employment.

The risks involved in learning

For men, therefore, particularly those who are unemployed, there can be considerable risks involved in participating in learning programmes: risks to their self-esteem, status and standing in the community; and risks to their financial survival. In their study of motivation, Hand, Gambles and Cooper (1994) found that the factor that most differentiates potential learners is the degree of risk they face at the point in their lives where they are considering undertaking learning. This obviously varies with individual circumstances and expectations. The risk is obviously less for those in relatively comfortable occupational and economic circumstances than for those undertaking learning to compensate for inability to work because of poor initial education, redundancy, ill health, parenthood or unsatisfactory working conditions. The researchers argue that individuals in the latter group need confidence in the effectiveness of learning to improve their situation and in their own ability to achieve the learning goals. Both of these are, to some extent, determined by their previous experience of education. For unemployed individuals, participation in an education and training programme may also risk doing further damage their quality of life and insecure finances. Those who do take the step also risk disappointment as they may expect more than education can deliver. Education may make them become more 'employable' but it cannot create more jobs.

• • •

There are, then, as one would expect, a wide range of interacting factors which cause male non-participation. Generally speaking these can be divided into factors which impede a person's readiness to engage in learning (cultural, social and psychological barriers) and factors which inhibit his or her ability to participate (practical and structural barriers). As the motivation to learn comes before the experiencing of barriers, it is often assumed that its absence represents the most powerful deterrent. However, adult participation is the result of a more complex process than individual motivation alone. It is the interaction of a whole swathe of cultural, structural and practical factors that brings some groups into education and keeps others out. An understanding of these should inform any approaches designed to increase their participation.

Table 33. Obstacles to learning by sex, by percentage

	All those no longer in full-time education	Men	Women
I prefer to spend my free time doing things other than learning	39	42	35
I'm not interested in doing any learning, training or education	16	17	16
I don't need to do any learning for the sort of work I want to do	15	16	13
I'm so busy with work, I don't have time to spend learning	29	34	25
I haven't got time because of my family	24	16	31
It is hard to get time off work to do any learning for my job	18	21	14
It is hard for me to pay the fees they charge for courses	21	18	26
I am only willing to do learning if the fees are paid by someone else	11	12	11
My benefits would be cut if I did a training course	5	4	6
I know very little about training opportunities around here	20	21	20
I want to do some learning, but can't find any opportunities locally	11	11	11
I don't have the qualifications you need to get on to most courses	15	13	17
I would be worried about keeping up with the other people on the course	13	10	17
I have difficulties with reading or writing	5	7	4
I have difficulties with English	4	5	4
I feel that I'm too old to learn	13	11	15
My health problems or disability make it difficult for me to do any learning	7	7	7
I did not enjoy learning at school	17	19	15
None of the statements applied to the respondent	13	14	12
Had taken part in a learning activiity in the past three years	74	78	70
Weighted base	5245	2589	2656
Unweighted base	5386	2466	2920

Source: National Adult Learning Survey, SCPR, 1997

Table 34. Employee training by age

Per cent

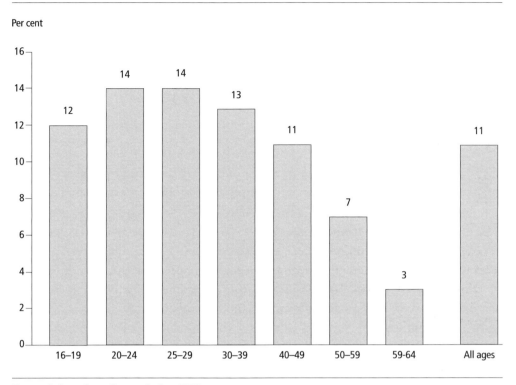

Source: *Labour Force Survey, Spring 1996*

Note: Men aged 16–64 and women aged 15–59.
This table refers to training provided/funded by employers.

Table 35. Employees receiving training by educational level

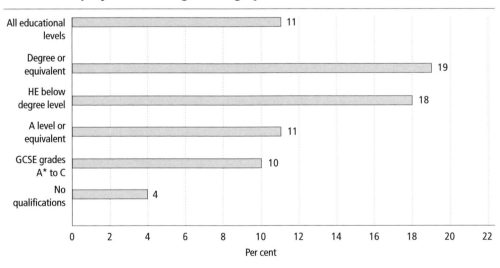

Source: *Labour Force Survey, Autumn 1996*

Note: Men aged 16-64 and women aged 15-59. This table refers to training provided/funded by employers

CHAPTER FOUR

Young men:
Examples of approaches
to improve motivation and
participation

The next challenges are how to overcome the barriers faced by many men, how to contact them and respond appropriately to their learning interests and needs. Do non-participating men require the same or different approaches from those that have proved effective with women? What recruitment methods and programmes work best with young men, working-class men, men from minority ethnic groups and those over 50?

Hand, Gambles, and Cooper (1994) found that many former non-learners become involved in learning for two main reasons: because of some kind of external compulsion (unemployment, the Benefits system, employer requirements) or because of a change in their personal circumstances (redundancy, divorce, retirement). The latter tendency was clearly demonstrated in the NIACE 1996 Gallup survey which found that 59 per cent of current and recent learners had moved house, 46 per cent had experienced a marriage break up and 45 per cent had lost a job (Sargant *et al*, 1997).

Despite evidence that a return to learning is associated with life change, the men least likely to engage in education and training are often those experiencing a period of change or transition: young men passing from adolescence to adulthood; those leaving school and trying to find their first job; men who have lost their job and men facing retirement.

Some claim that the whole male sex is currently going through a crisis of transition (although many men might dispute this): *'Men's changing role is no less stressful [than bereavement] even though it is not represented by a sudden event, but is taking place over a long period of time. The slow "death" of traditional masculinity also requires an emotional response although this is hard for many men, given their notorious "emotional illiteracy".'* (Baker, 1996: 33)

Education has a potentially crucial role in helping boys and men to manage these difficult transition periods if they can be persuaded of its value and relevance. However, those who leave school without qualifications often have little awareness of the critical link between educational achievement and employment prospects and associate learning with *'boredom, irrelevance and failure'* (Ball, 1991). Many men with basic skill needs fail to seek assistance and those who are jobless or facing redundancy do not usually consider learning their first priority. How to motivate these groups and change their perceptions of the value of education is therefore a key question.

Boys at school

Given current concerns about low-achieving and so-called 'disaffected' young men, it is logical to start with the school system, since it is schools which socialise young men into adulthood and what happens at school has a strong bearing on future attitudes to learning. At this stage the biggest challenge is to change the prevailing peer culture so that is no longer a stigma to be seen as a 'boff' and boys consider it acceptable to expend effort on their school work. This is an issue for the wider culture rather than schools alone. However, a start has been made with the range of national strategies, launched under the 'New Start' initiative, to improve achievement levels and make schooling more work-related and relevant to boys. It is particularly important to raise the aspirations of boys who come from a culture which does not value education.

Applying more varied assessment measures

One of the problems highlighted by gender disparities in GCSE results is that school performance in different subjects is evaluated according to a single standard of academic achievement, a situation exacerbated by the annual reporting of school league tables. This can make under-achievers (of both sexes) feel inadequate. The sense of failure felt by some individuals might be alleviated if there were intermediate assessment measures that recognised smaller achievements and distance travelled.

Some analysts suggest that giving more status to vocational learning in schools would help to resolve some of the tension between academic success and conceptions of masculinity (Seidler, 1996).

Improving core skills

The greatest concern of parents, teachers and policy-makers is the gap between boys and girls in their development of basic skills. A government-funded helpline for parents worried about their children's literacy levels which was piloted in Sunderland in 1997. This generated nearly 400 enquiries, three-quarters of which were about boys. The service is being launched nationally and will be expanded to include numeracy. A range of other national measures to improve children's basic skills have also been announced. New literacy and numeracy targets have been set for local education authorities: by the year 2002, 80 per cent of 11-year-olds will be expected to reach the appropriate standard for their age in reading and writing (in 1996, only 57 per cent achieved that standard), and 75 per cent will be required to reach the appropriate standards in numeracy. To help achieve the targets, a variety of out-of-school-hours learning schemes have been initiated with funding from the DfEE and some support from industry. These include homework clubs, family learning schemes, mentoring programmes and literacy luncheon clubs. Over 560 basic skills summer schools were organised in 1998.

One of the biggest problems identified is that boys regard English as a subject for girls. A report on improving boys' performance in English produced by the Qualifications and Curriculum Authority (QCA, 1998) suggests that while there are powerful cultural forces outside of teachers' control which shape boys' behaviour and attitudes, there are steps a school can take to improve their attainment levels. It is pointed out that the steady improvement in girls' academic performance over the years demonstrates what can be achieved when schools follow through a carefully targeted process designed to recognise problems and change practice and attitudes: *'The causes of the original under-achievement were analysed and described. Specific actions were then piloted and monitored and successful practice was disseminated. Pupils' perceptions of mathematics and science were examined and negative attitudes challenged; aspects of teaching and learning from planning through to assessment were rigorously analysed. The focus at every stage was at changing classroom practice. As a result, the expectations of staff and pupils shifted and there was a significant improvement in achievement. The broad lines of approach to this success can be adapted to other groups of pupils including boys.'* (QCA, 1998, 8).

The basic message of the QCA report is that schools need to counter the assumption that English is a girls' subject by adopting teaching and learning approaches that appeal more to boys. It is suggested that boys' reading and writing skills could be improved by an approach that takes account of the fact that they prefer activity to passive learning and respond more to non-fiction related to practical activities than to fiction and poetry (QCA, 1998). Studies have also found that the sexes prefer different styles of learning and assessment; girls prefer knowledge set in context while boys prefer their information abstract and out of context. Boys prefer tasks that give quick results and they often do better in one-to-one teaching relationships as their peer culture discourages them from volunteering answers or engaging in open-ended, shared tasks (Williams, 1996).

Single-sex teaching
Some schools have improved boys' achievement levels by teaching English in single-sex groups.

A secondary school in Winchester where, as elsewhere, boys have been getting lower GCSE results than girls, has piloted a boys-only English class for those under-achieving in English. A teacher who is also responsible for sports is in charge of the scheme, and lessons involve a more didactic teaching methodology than is normally employed, with course materials chosen specifically to appeal to boys. The intention is to create a team atmosphere where the boys support one another. According to one member of staff: *'when girls are present they are loath to express opinions for fear of appearing sissy – their instinct is to stay aloof and macho. If it's all boys together then it's much easier to break down inhibitions'*. This comment was confirmed in feedback from one boy: *'I like English now because there is less pressure … if you made a comment the other boys would make fun of you to make you look silly in front of the girls. Now we support each* *other. We are all working hard to show that we can be just as successful as other groups.'*

Although it was initially resisted by staff and pupils, the strategy has significantly raised standards. In 1996 the gap between boys' and girls' GCSE grades was 22 per cent; in 1997 this had fallen to one per cent. There are now plans to set up similar groups for maths and science.

The school has also set up a staff mentor scheme for under-achievers. The pupils and mentors meet every week to review progress and 84 per cent of them are now expected to achieve much higher grades as a result of the scheme (Redwood, 1998).

Involving football clubs

Boys' school progress can be improved by relating school work to their leisure interests. Many boys are passionately interested in football and in some areas this is being used to stimulate greater application to schoolwork. An English teacher at a London comprehensive school reports that the best course work she has received from boys studying for GCSE was when football and well-known players were the topic.

Some study support centres, within or near premier league club grounds, have been established to motivate under-achieving pupils in primary and secondary schools. They provide learning programmes in literacy, numeracy and information technology with costs covered by local education authorities, football clubs and businesses.

Using information technology

The potential of IT for helping under-achieving boys has perhaps not yet been fully explored. Many boys who are under-achieving in an academic sense are adept at, and enthusiastic about, using computers. This interest could be exploited to help improve their literacy and numeracy skills. It is often suggested that computer-aided learning is particularly suitable for boys and men: working on a computer is safe and private with no risk of humiliation or losing face. It provides rapid feedback and the results of one's work on screen or print-out look better than on a messy, hand-written page. This enhances the learner's self-esteem: *'If you look at the areas in which boys succeed you find that they are very very good at playing computer games, those zap-the-baddies exercises in high-speed wrist skills in which everything is reduced to the urge to pass from one level to another, to some final unseen reward (...) When the education ministry examines ways of challenging the male culture of the playground, it will have to look very carefully at the Playstation and instead of condemning it as a pernicious form of dumbing-down, ask why boys are willing to devote so many hours to sitting attentively in front of its screen, motivated, willing themselves to succeed, beating girls who are barely in the race.'* (Grant, 1998).

In the Harehills area of Leeds a community-based, information technology learning centre has been set up with the support of local businesses, for children who are not performing well at school. The centre offers help in basic education and maths and has attracted mainly young men and those from the black communities.

A comprehensive school in Bristol has intensified its basic skills programme to help under-achieving boys. The Successmaker software reading programme has been integrated into basic skills teaching and books likely to appeal to boys have been purchased for the school library. The local city football club has become involved in the scheme and well known local players have been invited to present books as prizes to boys. The school is now considering splitting the different achievement groups into single sex groups to raise standards among boys (Crace, 1998).

Providing male role models

Initiatives aimed at improving boys' achievement levels could usefully be supplemented by attempts to provide more older role models: *'We still have to acknowledge what socialisation means in the growth and development of boys (…) and the kind of nourishment and support that they might need from relationships with older men (…) It does not need to involve a father, but there should be a man – even an older student – who can be respected for his personal qualities and ability to share his life story and experience. Where there is uncertainty about what it means for boys to grow up into manhood, we need to open up a conversation between different generations in a way that can help boys feel good about themselves as young men.'* (Seidler, 1996: 119).

Under-achieving boys often come from families and communities where it is rare for men to participate in organised programmes of education or training, and fathers tend to be less actively involved in their children's education than mothers. This reinforces the impression that education is largely a feminine affair.

The appointment of more male teachers at both primary and secondary school level could help boys develop a more positive approach to learning. A research study in Wales (Woolford and McDougall, 1998) found that boys in classes with a male teacher had higher reading levels, a better vocabulary and knowledge than girls in the same class. Conversely, girls in a class with a female teacher did better than the boys. Since this was a small-scale study, the findings are tentative but they do suggest a relationship between achievement levels and the sex of the teacher.

Training older boys as mentors to assist and guide younger ones can also help raise achievement levels.

A Hampshire infant school has held a successful 'Bring a Dad to School Day', the idea being to close the gender gap (there are only two adult males at the school – a teacher and the caretaker); to get fathers or other male relatives more involved in school life and to provide positive examples to boys. One hundred and fifty men attended and both they and the pupils appeared to thoroughly enjoy the experience (Barnard, 1998b).

With support from the Extending Learning Communities fund, the **London Borough of Waltham Forest Adult Education Service** has run several introductory computer courses for men and their sons (aged 7-13). These have proved very popular. There has been 100 per cent attendance and the men have expressed appreciation for this kind of cross-generational learning. (Information supplied by Mary Crowley, Waltham Forest Education.)

Nottingham Garibaldi Comprehensive has introduced a mentoring scheme for boys. When they start at the school, boys are mentored by 16-year-old boys who are themselves led through the GCSE process and into A level work by sixth-formers acting as mentors. The boys are matched up according the football teams they support and they meet for 40 minutes a week without formal supervision. For those in year 7 the scheme reduces the fear of older boys and worries about being bullied.

Providing a more relevant curriculum

It might also help under-achieving boys if the relevance of what they were learning could be demonstrated in a real life context.

Children from a deprived area of Rochdale with high male unemployment are being encouraged to take a greater interest in maths as a result of an innovative scheme which demonstrates the relevance of the subject in a local factory – a plant that makes cleaning, materials and toiletries.

Pupils in every school year have visited the factory to study different aspects of manufacturing. They then made presentations to their tutor groups to explain what they had learned. The groups examined aspects of the way maths was used at the factory. They studied how volume was measured and the importance of such measurements in a bottling plant. They also considered relevant environmental issues.

The partnership with the factory has had a number of beneficial spin-offs. The visits have enabled children to see the importance of maths in solving practical problems and have helped to raise achievement levels in the subject. The school has started using more mental arithmetic in teaching and is adopting a whole-school approach in which children are shown the relevance of maths in every subject (Edwards, 1997a).

Some feel that schooling insufficiently prepares children for adult life and that there should be greater stress in the curriculum on helping boys to understand changing gender and work roles and preparing them for a future in which employment will be only one part of their life: *'The starting point has to be to help men, from an early stage, to reflect on what they want from their lives and on the importance of having a spread of investments — not only in paid work, not only in leisure interests, not only in public life, but also in family life and in relationships with partners and children.'* (Moss, 1996: 247).

This means that there should be greater emphasis on skills for parenthood, particularly for boys: *'Greater encouragement of fathering could come through education. Some young offenders' institutions already give boys training in parenting skills and there is no obvious reason why these programmes should not be made more widely available. There cannot be many schools currently teaching their male students how to sterilise a bottle, purée soft fruits and burp a baby.'* (Baker, 1996: 37).

In working-class communities there used to be little link between what was learnt at school and the kind of jobs available for young men. This situation has changed radically but school-based research suggests that many boys still expect to obtain manual jobs on leaving school and lead a traditional lifestyle in which they will engage in continuous employment while their partners stay at home and look after children and household. They also expect to have power over female partners in any future relationships rather than a more equal partnership (Riddell, 1992).

Some believe that there should also be a greater emphasis in schools on helping boys to understand some of the problems they face during key stages of development. This might involve exploring with them issues such as violence, sexism, racism and homophobia, and helping them to respect diversity and difference and to develop alternative ways of dealing with conflict. Lloyd (1996) has found that young men will respond to discussion about such matters if the adults working with them are well trained and sufficiently skilled to protect them from mutual ridicule and banter. This has implications for teacher training.

A training module which has been pioneered in South Australia – **'The Boys and Relationships Programme'** – is designed to help teachers address the gender issues that can have a negative impact on boys' school performance.

The module examines what it is like to be male in a context of high male unemployment and discusses ways of encouraging boys to see education as something valuable in its own right. It raises awareness of male conditioning and how it influences behaviour and learning at school. There are exercises and role play which aim to help teachers deal with boys' behaviour in ways other than trying to win every power struggle (Lane, 1998).

Working with boys from minority ethnic communities

Some initiatives have been set up specifically to raise standards among boys from African-Caribbean communities, the group most likely to be excluded from school.

A number of **supplementary Saturday schools** have been set up in Afro-Caribbean and other minority ethnic communities around the country, in response to parents' frustration with mainstream state schooling and the perceived low expectations teachers have of black children. The schools are community-funded and run by volunteers. They provide the kind of learning support parents feel is missing in state schools in a setting where black, rather than white, is the norm. The focus is not only on the national curriculum but also on cultural background. An evaluation of black supplementary education conducted by researchers at South Bank University found that, although the Saturday schools start from the three Rs, teachers use the children's own culture as a starting point for learning. This raises motivation and aspirations, and there is little disruptive behaviour. In many of the schools, parents and school sign a contract setting out rights and responsibilities (Barnard, 1997a; Julius, 1998).

As a result of a collaboration between the **Afro-Caribbean Network for Science and Technology and Liverpool Hope University College**, young people aged 11-18 from minority ethnic communities in Toxteth are offered access to the multi-media suite and laboratories on the university campus. The scheme is aimed mainly at African-Caribbean young people who suffer from negative stereotyping in schools. The young people attend the Liverpool Ishango Club which runs after-school classes to improve attainment in maths and science and they can use the university facilities on Saturday mornings. The university, which has a very low number of black science undergraduates, provides some financial and administrative support for the scheme. The aims are to raise confidence and aspirations among those not previously motivated to study science and to encourage a long-term learning culture among those who have been disaffected from mainstream schooling (Millar, 1998).

City College Manchester is developing a school mentoring project supporting African-Caribbean and Asian boys in school. The aim is to raise confidence, self-esteem and achievement levels and reduce the number of exclusions from school in this community.

Disruptive or non-attending pupils

A range of schemes have been set up across the country to try and reduce truancy and the number of exclusions of boys.

A joint education/social services project has been set up in Salford for pupils in their last year of school. They can attend part-time education in social services premises, attend college or work placements for the rest of the week and also participate in Outward Bound training run by a voluntary organisation. The scheme is characterised by a high teacher:pupil ratio and an informal atmosphere. In 1994-95, over 50 per cent of participants with an offending record went on to a job, college or training place.

Younger pupils at risk of exclusion are also offered part-time support in schools or community settings by teachers involved in the joint project. All pupils who make use of the service have time set aside each week for one-to-one counselling and help with developing individual action plans (Audit Commission, 1996).

Cities in Schools works with young people who have been excluded from school and those with school attendance and behavioural problems. The aim is to address underlying problems, rebuild self-esteem and re-integrate them into mainstream education and training.

The scheme operating in South Glamorgan runs four programmes. These include:

Bridge courses for pupils in year 11: a personal tutor organises a weekly programme for pupils who are not attending school. This includes two days at a local further education college; two days spent on work-related experience and one day divided between a tutorial and structured leisure time. Individual progress is reviewed every 12 weeks. The personal tutor liaises with the family, care provider and other agencies and generally acts as a mentor. The aims are to help young people improve their literacy, numeracy and life skills, develop constructive leisure interests and explore career options, and to help provide positive alternatives to care and custody.

Bridge courses for year 10 pupils whose education has broken down. These courses aim to create positive attitudes to education and either to re-integrate young people into mainstream education or to prepare them for a year 11 Bridge course. The arrangements are similar to the year 11 course, with up to 10 pupils on the course at one time and a personal tutor in charge of the programme.

A re-integration project for pupils who are not attending mainstream school due to exclusion or long-term non-attendance. This aims to re-integrate young people into school as rapidly as possible by providing temporary programmes which address individual problems and barriers to learning. Each pupil is given an agreed target date for full-time transfer and a staged re-integration programme.

Attendance on Bridge courses has averaged over 80 per cent, in comparison with 39 per cent in the students' previous schools. In 1995-96, 90 per cent of the students who completed year 11 courses had a positive first destination with 36 per cent going on to youth training; 10 per cent to employment and 28 per cent to further education. Attitudes to education and employment had improved considerably, as had self-confidence and self-esteem. Students' reactions to the scheme have been largely positive (Audit Commission, 1996).

The Schools Project in South London is an addition to Lambeth Employment Training Scheme (LETS), a programme running Network training funded through Youth Credits for those over the age of 16. The programme offers a second chance to 15-year-olds who are not doing well at school, and takes on 60 young people at a time. The pupils (who remain on their school rolls) enter a roll-on, roll-off programme providing help with maths, English, science, and vocational skills such as painting and decorating, catering, motor mechanics and childcare. The teaching staff already work with the over 16 age group and are used to relating to young people as tutors rather than as school teachers.

As the project is located with a Network scheme, students have access to workshop provision in a range of skill areas taught by experienced tutors. They also have an older age cohort to mix with. This makes them aware of the kind of progression possibilities available after the age of 16.

Feedback from participants has been very positive. They like the fact that the scheme is different from school, with teachers who are approachable and lenient. They treat students like adults and are more caring. Classes are smaller, they have more tutor attention and are given one-to-one help when needed. The more relaxed atmosphere of the project and absence of uniform or fuss about clothes are also appreciated. The fact that they have chosen to attend the scheme leads to commitment (Maclagen, 1997b).

Two further education colleges, **Manchester College of Arts and Technology** and **City College**, are running sixth forms and post-16 centres in secondary schools in deprived areas of Manchester. The aim is to reduce massive drop-out rates by providing courses in a familiar environment as it has been found that some young people are intimidated by further education colleges. However, students in the sixth form have access to college resources. A one-year pilot that preceded the scheme brought about a 6 per cent rise in staying-on rates (Nash, 1997c).

The Further Education Development Agency (FEDA) has produced a guide to help colleges to reach out to poorly motivated young people. This addresses support issues and stresses the need for an earmarked budget, an adult and caring environment, and an integrated approach to 14-19 provision involving diagnosis of need and action planning. The report recommends that colleges provide a variety of activities and subjects that are different from those provided in school, with regular progress monitoring and rewards for achievement. It also stresses the need for staff to address students' personal as well as academic development and to treat students with respect.

Young men who have left school

Unqualified and unemployed male school-leavers are one of the most difficult groups to reach by statutory agencies, although they may not be isolated in a literal sense: *'How can young people, who are on the streets selling drugs, drinking alcohol, stealing cars or eking out an existence doing all sorts of "fiddly" jobs in the "informal economy", be said to be excluded from their communities?'* (Coffield, 1997: 85).

Attracting this group to further education or training is not easy. Although many have poor basic skills they are likely to be sceptical about the value of education which they see as having little relevance to them. If asked about their learning needs, most disaffected young men would say they do not need education or training, they need a job (Midgeley, 1997b). The health project targeted at young men in Northern Ireland confirmed that work is very important to them as it provides a role, status and income. Similarly, when over 100 young people on supervision orders were asked what might stop them offending, the most frequent response was a job, followed by sport and other leisure activities (Audit Commission, 1996).

Despite their interest in work, however, it is frequently found that many unemployed young men have little awareness of the realities of the labour market. A survey of centres providing careers advice and of a sample of their clients revealed that among school and college leavers, high achievers and girls had realistic expectations whereas low achievers and most boys, especially those in poor communities, did not (Nash, 1997a). Although the careers service draws up an action plan for school pupils two years before they leave, recording achievements, goals and training needs, persistent truants and those who have been excluded from school often miss out on this service and therefore receive no advice to help them gain an informed understanding of the changing labour market. Once out in the adult world, their chances of gaining this information are slim. White (1990) has pointed out how difficult it is for young unemployed people without qualifications or job experience to obtain information about labour market opportunities as they lack access to 'inside' information.

The Audit Commission (1996) suggests that young men 'on the margins' would have a better chance of entering further education, training or employment if there were systematic attempts by the careers and youth services, working in collaboration, to identify and contact them and offer careers advice at all levels of ability.

National initiatives

Concern about young people who leave school at 16 without qualifications and fail to engage in employment, further education and training has led to the setting up a ministerial group, chaired by the Home Secretary, Jack Straw. A number of national initiatives have also been launched to help this group. Unemployed 16- and 17-year-olds can now enter one of three programmes: the pre-vocational New Start programme which is designed to improve literacy, numeracy and presentation skills; National Traineeships which by autumn 1998 are expected to cover as many as 50 sectors, and which include basic skills, specific industry skills and the opportunity to work towards National Vocational Qualification (NVQ) level 2; and Modern Apprenticeships which lead to NVQ level 3. Legislation is also planned to establish an entitlement for unqualified employees aged 16 to have paid time off to study or train for a NVQ level 2 or its equivalent.

For those aged 18-24, the New Deal offers a period of help and advice in a Gateway guidance programme and four options including subsidised employment, voluntary work, attachment to an environmental task force or up to a year in full-time education with an allowance. There are already signs that the majority of unqualified young men prefer employment to education and training. In the first two months after the New Deal was launched in 12 'pathfinder' areas, nearly three-quarters of participants chose employment rather than full-time training or other options (although jobs include a guarantee of one day's training a week) (Midgeley, 1997b). The 23 per cent who went into education or training did so mainly at a basic skills level.

Involving unemployed young men in training

For training programmes to attract young people, they need to be seen as an opportunity rather than a penalty and as a route to more substantial employment outcomes than previous programmes have provided: *The long series of schemes of Youth Training failed to produce a high quality track from school to work and for too many proved a dead end without access to employment or further learning.'* (Coffield (1997: 9).

Young men who have participated in a succession of schemes without noticeable benefit to their situation or prospects may understandably be sceptical about the value of training. Since their first priority is a job, programmes with work placements and guaranteed job interviews are the most likely to attract them. Maclagen (1997b) argues that it is not appropriate to provide young people who have never had paid employment with short-term training as this might be seen as preparing them for a casualised labour market. They require longer programmes that replicate the world of work as closely as possible. However, many young men in this situation have personal or educational difficulties which preclude direct entry to a training programme. They need to achieve a degree of emotional health and stability in their lives before they can become effective learners (NIACE/NYA, 1998). According to the director of the charity, Youthaid: to force young people who are not ready into training would be *like trying to force a square peg into a round hole'* (Chatrik 1997a).

Rolfe, Bryson and Metcalf (1996) suggest that models such as the 'taster and tester' courses offered by some Training and Enterprise Councils

(TECs) in the recent past would be of value to young people with little experience of employment or training, especially if they include in-depth guidance to help individuals choose and prepare for appropriate programmes. They regret that this kind of provision has been curtailed because of funding cuts. Regret has also been expressed at the cutting of training hours in TEC provision since those with the greatest learning needs require more rather than less time to achieve satisfactory results: *'They are already less attractive to training providers trying to make money or even to stay afloat, and the lessening of hours might remove a useful safeguard or lead to less training, time, attention and support being offered to those who need it most.'* (Maclagen, 1997b).

It can take time for disaffected young people, especially those in difficult circumstances, to adapt to training and employment programmes, and New Deal arrangements need to take account of this. Tuckett (1997) quotes Clara Donnelly of the Unemployment Unit on this point: *'not everyone in the target group will find it easy to develop overnight the disciplines of the timetable of the working day. For providers, matching flexibility and sensitivity to learners with the need to meet the rules may be the key to a programme that genuinely transforms work prospects for people'.*

Those working with unemployed and disaffected young people have found that their problems and barriers to learning are best overcome when all relevant agencies – youth services, the Employment Service, the Benefits Agency, social services, the probation service, careers services, TECs, further education colleges, and other education and training providers – work together in a coordinated strategy to help them (Merton, 1997b).

Devising appropriate programmes for disaffected young people

Merton (1997a) calls for provision of properly resourced programmes for young people which take account of their circumstances. These should have both structure and flexibility, allowing for some content to be negotiated within a clear framework.

There is some unanimity on the objectives of learning programmes for this group: *'[they] should equip young people with the key skills, attitudes and behaviours which will enable them to become more independent learners and better able to cope with an unpredictable labour market and with difficulties at home and in the community.'* (Merton 1997b). The educational element in youth work has been defined as: *'the learning, growth (to maturity) and development of participative and social skills that are transferable to enable involvement in society at large'.* (Lloyd, 1996: 54). This suggests that educational strategies for disaffected young men need to cover in equal measure, basic and key skills and personal and social skills. For young people without experience of employment, these need to be developed in a context that helps them to adapt to the disciplines of a work routine.

Key skills At a series of regional consultations, the key skills required by young people outside employment and education were identified as:
- reading, writing, calculating and communicating effectively

- developing self-awareness, particularly of strengths and needs
- accessing information and advice
- handling authority
- working in teams
- planning use of time and other resources
- negotiating agreements
- knowing how the system works – opportunities and constraints
- making decisions and taking responsibility for their consequences
- solving problems
- resolving conflict
- coping with stress and tension
- reviewing progress, recording achievements and improving on performance
- taking part in dialogue
- thinking for oneself
- dealing with change
- using IT
- developing practical skills such as driving and
- first-aid. (Merton, 1997b)

Personal and social skills The Young Adult Learners' Project (YALP) is designing a curriculum framework that is intended to address attitudes, feelings and behaviour as much as knowledge and understanding. The curriculum proposes to develop the following skills:
- developing self-awareness and self-esteem
- holding values, beliefs and attitudes
- coping with feelings
- handling relationships
- exercising rights and responsibilities
- exploring risks and their consequences
- asking for help and support
- managing resources
- finding and using information

'The task is then to create a set of themes or projects related to young people's interests and experiences through which these skills can be taught and learned at different levels of difficulty and complexity.' (NIACE/NYA, 1998)

Programme structure It is recommended that programmes incorporating these elements be structured in a modular way and organised in: *'"bite-size chunks", each with measurable learning outcomes on which young people can build'* (Merton 1997a).

One-to-one work Lloyd (1996) advises that programmes for young men should incorporate some one-to-one work as they tend to avoid self-disclosure in a group situation. In the health education project in Northern

Ireland, for example, it was found that they were uncomfortable and some-times disruptive and abusive when workers tried to draw them into serious discussion. There was, however, a dramatic difference between young men in public (when their mates were around) and in private (when they were on their own with a worker). In the former situation, discussion was often disrupted and those who attempted to participate were ridiculed or 'slagged off'. In a one-to-one situation, individuals were more willing to discuss the issues affecting their lives.

It has been found that young men do not necessarily want unstructured learning programmes. Despite their apparently negative attitude to school, they prefer a controlled framework and environment in which to learn: '*Some (...) are often attracted to very structured and formal environments such as football, boxing and the military. Their resistance to school is more often about content, their ability to relate to the content, their general confidence towards school work and the style of structure and formality. Workers often confuse these and fail to contain the environment for young men (the containment often providing the safety the young men need to be able to engage and get involved).*' (Lloyd, 1996: 25)

Attracting young men to learning programmes

Designing appropriate programmes is one thing; recruiting disaffected young men to them is quite another matter. It is often found that this group are reluctant to attend formal institutions. According to Merton (1997b), they prefer a non-threatening learning environment in which they can enjoy relationships of trust, direct and honest communication with older adults: '*Institutional responses fail to win the confidence of disaffected young people.*'

A project in Gloucestershire involving Whitbreads Brewery targets young men on a large estate via three pubs. They are offered courses in areas such as sports leadership and technology.

Once contact has been made and interest aroused, educational responses to young men need to be prompt and on the spot. According to a probation officer, it is no good '*sending them off on a bus to the college*' as this will have no results. One needs to engage them, there and then, on the spot.

Cash incentives
Unemployed young men will sometimes enrol in programmes that offer financial assistance or incentives such as meals:

The Basic Skills Service at Pontypridd College realised that it was failing to attract young people aged 18+ who were not involved in employment or training programmes. In an attempt to rectify this situation it collaborated with Mid Glamorgan TEC in devising a new accredited scheme for this group, based on the Training for Work framework but including special incentives and rewards.

The programme had the following features:

- participants were required to attend for 15 hours a week (and could stay for up to 52 weeks) and each would agree a personal action plan;
- participants would receive £10 a week on top of state benefits and all travel expenses;
- they would also receive a reward of £50 payable on completion of their first Wordpower award and a further £50 for their first Numberpower award.

Publicity and referral sources included the Employment Service, Job Centres, Job Clubs, community groups and word of mouth. Recruitment was *'amazingly easy: the cash incentives which seemed very modest to us had magical powers. The TEC had agreed 40 places and we filled them within a month'*.

Participants spent a core of six hours per week in intensive small group tuition in either communications or numeracy and nine hours per week in guided learning to do with anything agreed in their action plans. The course included vocational tasters, visiting speakers, outside visits and job search at Job Centres or Job Clubs. Participants also had access to college drop-in workshops, the town centre open learning centre and IT training sessions.

All elements of the programme had built-in incentives. Lunch was included during outside visits and buffet meals were provided after presentations of awards. Students were presented with college certificates on completion of tasks as well as *Computers don't Bite* certificates which were *'much appreciated by people who had never received any formal acknowledgement of their achievements'*.

This approach has led to a 94 per cent retention rate and some progression to other college courses and jobs, although it was found that many students needed a more extended period of support. The greatest achievement, however, was the visible change in attitudes among participants: *'The biggest thrill of all, we see real attitudinal change. Initially some are very defensive or sullen. They like us to know that they are here on their terms, for the money etc. Literally within a month we hear none of this. Sullen faces disappear. Students look us fully in the face. They smile, they laugh. They turn up early. We can honestly say that cash incentives 'hook' our learners but this motivation very quickly recedes and a genuine enjoyment of the programme takes over.'* (Morgan, 1997)

City College Manchester has been using European Social Fund (ESF) money to provide free courses for young unemployed people who otherwise would not be able to afford to attend. Students receive £10 a week for travel expenses on top of benefits. In 1996, two pilot courses were run in computer skills and watch-making and no-one dropped out. In 1997 there were about 40 vocational courses with job search for unemployed individuals to choose from (Russell 1997).

In 1996, 12 per cent of 16-year-olds in Coventry were jobless. Among these were a hard core of alienated young people many of whom had been involved in crime. **Quality Careers in Coventry** organises outreach activities targeted specifically at unemployed youths and runs a project called Breakthrough which pays young people up to £15 a day to go on one-day taster courses or work placements. In 1996 over half of 180 participants were helped into jobs or training. The company also sends careers advisers to schools (Edwards, 1997b).

Capitalising on expressed interests and needs

Learning programmes targeted at young men must be relevant to their circumstances and interests. A common approach is to ask groups to identify favourite activities and use these as a starting point. However, this runs the risk of eliciting a limited response based on what are seen as appropriate masculine activities. There is also a related problem of how to move young men on from enjoyable activities to serious learning. Lloyd (1996) reports that one of the most common issues raised by youth workers is the difficulty of moving young men beyond the informal sport and activity base into learning: *'Most models of youth work rely on the worker to identify need: here lies a problem with work with boys and young men. If it is predominately active and sports based, if young men see the provision as only this, then when asked about their needs they are likely to express only their physical needs. The nature of masculinity also plays its part here: 'real men' do not have learning needs or express concerns. This makes the identification of needs subject to the process issue. If young men perceive youth provision as a place to play sport (with no educational content) and workers are looking to offer educational input on the back of sport and activity, there will inevitably be problems!'* (Lloyd 1996: 57-58).

Lloyd argues that although physical activities provide an effective way of attracting and involving young men, they can lead to the neglect of other curriculum areas. For example, getting them to engage in health-enhancing sport is easy, but getting them to reflect on the things they do that may be bad for their health is significantly harder. It requires real skill on the part of teachers and youth workers to lead young men from physical activity into a broader learning situation. Nevertheless, those with experience and expertise have successfully used young men's interest in sports, music, motor bikes and cars to improve their literacy and key skills.

The Newham Docklands Motorcycle Project in East London has introduced young people, mainly boys and young men, to vocational and key skills through their interest in motor bikes.

The Skilled Project run by the **Community Education Development Council** was supported by the National Literacy Trust and funded by News International. It used the combined skills of youth workers and basic skills tutors in projects that aimed to encourage disadvantaged young adults to develop their literacy and numeracy skills through practical activities such as driving, music, boat-building and making a radio programme.

Nine projects were run across Britain during the spring and summer of 1997. These used popular activities as a carrot to attract young people with low literacy levels who were then involved in programmes leading to accreditation in basic skills.

One of the nine projects, in the London Borough of Bexley, linked literacy with driving lessons. Participants were given help with literacy while they learned the theory and also received 10 free driving lessons. Thirty-four people aged 17 to 25 took part, attending one session a week for 15 weeks: 'They realised driving lessons was a carrot but didn't seem to mind too much.' As well as driving lessons there were activities such as go-karting, attending a car auction and information from the police about drinking and driving (Edwards, 1997d).

Many young men enjoy using computers and providing courses in information and communications technology can be another effective way of attracting them: *'Computers are very important. They are one of the ways people can begin to engage with what they see as the cutting edge of society. Hitherto they have seen themselves as completely separate from society, so when they begin to develop skills with computers that gives them messages about their own potential.'* (Midgley, 1997c)

Staff-student relationships

It goes without saying that the effectiveness of any approach depends on the skills and expertise of tutors and youth workers. The project in Northern Ireland revealed that young men attached great importance to being treated with respect and like an adult. The project was most effective when, amongst other things:

- aims and objectives were narrow, focused and achievable;
- young men were given responsibility and expected to acted responsibly;
- workers approached young men knowing what they would be interested in and what they would get involved in;
- workers were able to recognise and communicate to the young men the role they would have and any differences there may be from their usual roles;
- there was no hidden agenda (Lloyd, 1996).

Lloyd (1996: 59) warns workers to resist the temptation of acting as 'one of the lads': *'Some workers believe that unless they "get in with" young men they can't be effective. This can lead them to compete with young men (through activities, banter or use of power) in an attempt to gain the young men's respect. Alternatively, they may also become very tolerant of abusive or disruptive behaviour, often accepting this as "boys being boys". Workers have found that these approaches have led to compromises, either of their position as workers, or of their trusting adult status both of which are essential when developing work with young men.'* (Lloyd, 1996: 59)

Lloyd also stresses the importance of workers having a clear understanding of masculine conditioning and the 'proving' elements it involves. He points out that young men will fall along a spectrum of risk-taking and proving and that this will determine both the methods used and the outcomes that are achievable with them.

Continuity of support

Some workers claim that there is a problem not just with attracting young men to education programmes but with persuading them to stay. Sometimes they are attracted away into dead-end, short-term jobs. A grant or allowance attached to programmes may help this problem but tutors also need to raise awareness of the value of education and the fact that higher level skills will lead to more sustainable work.

Projects working with this group often find they need to continue providing support since some young men who have ostensibly left the programme to take up work return after a short period. Adult mentoring is one way of providing continuing support.

> **The Dalston Youth project** in East London assigns young people at risk to adult mentors who support them for at least a year in education, training or employment.

Schemes that help young people back into education, training and employment

A range of schemes throughout the country have been helping young people with no qualifications and skills, including the homeless and young offenders, to progress into employment or training schemes. While most are targeted at both sexes, the majority of the client group are young men.

> One of the pilot New Start projects which helps unqualified young people with poor basic skills to enter training or employment is the **Second Chance School** which was launched in Leeds in March 1998. The school is part of the East Leeds Family Learning Centre which already has a good record of attracting people from disadvantaged communities into learning. The informal centre which also has staff from the youth and community service, offers training programmes linked to local employment, a wide range of full- and part-time courses and the Duke of Edinburgh Award Scheme.

Liverpool Artskills operates in some of the most deprived areas of the European Union and is targeted at unqualified and unemployed young people who have failed at school and whom other statutory agencies have been unable to help. They are offered tuition in computing, art and vocational skills – painting, print-making, drama and performance skills, creative computer design, desktop publishing – at a range of sites in South Liverpool. The aim is to help them to move into further training or get a job.

According to the development manager, the scheme has been 'astonishingly successful' since its inception in February 1996. In that year, 90 per cent of those on the course acquired qualifications equivalent to level 1 or 2 of an NVQ; 65 per cent went on to do some form of further training or education; 19 per cent got jobs and 9 per cent went on to do voluntary work in the community: 'The outlook of the students has been transformed from one of demotivatlon and disempowerment to expanded horizons, optimism and motivation about what they can achieve.' (Midgley, 1997c).

Drive for Youth is a charity that aims to provide young unemployed people with the skills and confidence to find work. Each year it runs up to nine 22-week courses in personal development and employment-based training for 18-24 year-olds. Groups of 20-30 spend five weeks at the charity's training centre in Snowdonia. Here they work in teams of up to 12, exploring strengths and weaknesses via discussion and outdoor activities such as mountain treks, camping, abseiling and canoeing. Trainees are encouraged to become independent learners and to develop interpersonal skills, a sense of personal responsibility and leadership qualities. Every team member is required to find work experience placements to improve employability and they receive individual counselling on career options. At the end of the course each receives a City and Guilds Record of Achievement. The charity has a good record in helping and motivating young men, many of whom manage to obtain jobs after participating in the courses (Midgeley, 1997a).

The Weston Spirit which operates in inner city areas provides information and assistance in finding employment or training and encourages 16- and 17-year-olds to engage in positive and constructive activities.

The scheme running in Newcastle began in 1987, financed mainly by trusts and City Challenge and government grants. It assists around 70 young people each year, many of whom have been persistent truants or excluded from school. Most have been using drugs and 65 per cent have been cautioned or convicted for offending.

Young people are contacted through youth clubs, schools, outreach workers and word of mouth among their friends. Those interested in joining attend an introductory day, followed by a residential week in which they engage in team-building games and outdoor activities. For many participants, this is their first time away from their home environment.

After the week away, participants engage in educational and social activities such as constructing CVs, developing enterprise skills, drama, art and voluntary work. They can also drop in for information, advice or counselling. Many of them become involved in community action with groups such as disadvantaged children or elderly people. All of their achievements are accredited towards a City and Guilds qualification.

Participants also work on physical coordination and particularly dance which is popular because it relates to rock and pop culture. Working towards a performance is an important motivator and families are invited to take an interest and attend performances. Some participants have been accepted on further education dance courses.

Those who participate are expected to attend a full programme lasting from eight to 12 weeks. Although optional, attendance is over 70 per cent, especially among older participants and males. Since the scheme began, 90 per cent of participants have progressed to other things, 42 per cent into employment and 47 per cent to further education.

Some are offenders, referred by probation or social services. A national evaluation showed that only 5 per cent involved in the scheme subsequently offended. The majority of all participants have significantly raised their expectations and changed their attitudes (Audit Commission, 1996: 78-79).

Dr B's Caribbean Restaurant in Chapeltown, Leeds, is an initiative run by Barnardo's which helps unemployed young people aged 16-28 who would not make it onto a mainstream catering course to train for jobs in the catering industry. The scheme takes 15 trainees at a time, many of whom have a history of failure at school, and poverty and abuse at home. Trainees spend two years at the restaurant, in the kitchens and front of house, and work towards NVQ 1 and 2 in food preparation and cooking. They also spend eight weeks on placement in Leeds restaurants and hotel kitchens. Help with literacy skills and counselling is provided where necessary. Seventy per cent of trainees go on to find jobs in the catering industry (Wallace, 1998).

Double Take is a project targeted at young adults who are not in contact with the careers service or other sources of help and advice: '*even a modern careers office can be an intimidating place to some young people*'. It is funded by Warwickshire Careers Service in partnership with Coventry and Warwick TEC and receives some financial support from the Coal Plan Fund. As part of the scheme, experienced careers officers provide individual support and group activities on a careers service bus which visits disadvantaged housing areas. Young people can also obtain advice in their homes, shopping centres and cafés. Those who participate are encouraged to identify their aspirations and support needs and are given help in finding suitable training and employment opportunities. They are also offered training in job application and interviewing skills.

The project networks with other agencies in setting strategic goals and makes maximum use of available resources. It collaborates with local colleges, training providers and employers to develop a programme of tasters and work shadowing. To ensure that methods are appropriate, young people are represented on the steering group.

By the end of the first year ending in March 1995, the project had worked with 360 young people, many with poor basic skills and few formal qualifications. They included individuals who had been persistent truants or excluded from school, ex-offenders, young people with moderate learning difficulties, young people in very difficult circumstances, those who had been in care and lone parents. One hundred and sixty-three subsequently found work or training. However, some of these required continuing support as their employment or training placements only lasted for a short period.

Early on in the project the need for a central meeting place was identified and in the second year Hatter Space, a drop-in centre in Nuneaton, was opened with funding from community partners and charitable trusts. The centre is open one day a week and offers sports and leisure facilities as well as activities that encourage independent living and job search skills. Young people can suggest additional activities themselves (*Insight*, No 38, Spring 1997).

The Prince's Trust encourages young people to do voluntary work in their communities. The initiative started in 1990 with 10 pilots and now runs in about 150 locations with the support of a range of partners such as the Young Men's Christian Association (YMCA), fire services, Scottish Power, further education colleges, universities, community groups and youth organisations. The Trust is financed from a variety of sources – Government, TECs, the Further Education Funding Council (FEFC), other local services, and employers who buy places on the schemes.

Participants are involved for three months during which they come together in groups of 15 and devise projects to help their local community. These have included work with people who are disabled and have special needs; work in hospices, schools and day centres; out of school activities such as helping with homework clubs and peer mentoring (for example, working with under-achievers in schools). These activities require a range of key skills – communication, teamwork, decision-making and problem-solving. Each volunteer receives a City and Guilds Record of Achievement and their skills are accredited towards an NVQ.

In June 1997, more than 9000 16- to 25-year-olds volunteered to participate, an almost 50 per cent increase on the previous year. Many were unemployed and the scheme has an excellent record in raising their levels of self-esteem and confidence and helping them to gain a job or enter training. A MORI poll found that 12 months after their involvement, 77 per cent of all participants were either working or in education and training. The scheme's effectiveness in helping unemployed young people has been partly attributed to the fact that volunteers come from different environments and backgrounds. They are not all unemployed but include some individuals in full-time education and employment (for example, Marks and Spencer sees the scheme as a way of enabling sales and operations assistants to develop skills like planning and teamwork and gain a broadening experience). The mix of participants exposes unemployed young people to different outlooks and possibilities (Nash, 1997b).

Help for the most vulnerable groups

Some young people are in very difficult circumstances and require special support in order to enter training or employment.

Homeless young people

For homeless young people, learning will not be a priority: their first needs are for accommodation, employment and an income. Contacting them can be very difficult. Although a number of different agencies are involved with the homeless, there is not always a single, first point of contact and the relevant agencies do not have shared systems for recording contacts and interventions. For interventions to be successful, young homeless people need familiar people whom they can trust and relate to. These can be special workers or mentors. As an extension to the New Deal, a pilot programme has been announced involving a mentoring service for the most disadvantaged young people. This will involve volunteers from businesses, charities, churches and minority ethnic organisations who will act as personal advisers or 'buddies' to homeless individuals. The latter will also be offered access to specialised help to tackle homelessness, debt, drug and alcohol abuse.

With the backing of North Yorkshire TEC, **York College of Further and Higher Education** runs a special centre – The Lycett Centre – for young people aged 16-18 who are in difficult circumstances such as the homeless and ex-offenders. The approach is to tackle immediate needs, such as accommodation, with the help of the social services and other agencies, then to discuss individuals' longer term requirements. Once some kind of stability is achieved, tutors working within the NVQ options scheme, try to encourage participants into education, training or work. They work with Job Centres and local employers to find placements. The young people attend college one day a week and spend four days with an employer. It is found that many prefer work without training. Placements tend to be with smaller companies such as shops, garages or offices.

According to the scheme's coordinator, about half of participants in 1996, all people once seen as unemployable, progressed into work, training or further education (Crequer, 1997).

A survey conducted for **FOCUS**, the central London TEC, showed that it is even harder for young people to get jobs if they are homeless than if they have a criminal record. Since 1996, the TEC has led an initiative called 'Off the Streets and into Work' which provides skills development, training and jobs for single homeless people in central London. By summer 1997, the scheme had helped 386 homeless people get jobs (44 per cent of them from minority ethnic communities) and 300 had improved their prospects through training (Training Tomorrow, September, 1977).

Foyers provide an integrated approach to accommodation, training and employment for young people who are homeless and unemployed. There are about 60 foyers in Britain, each with its own source of income from a range of sources – government departments, national charities, European sources, TECs, Single Regeneration Budget (SRB), the Housing Corporation and the Lottery.

Foyers employ a holistic approach to young people. They provide vocational and personal guidance, and assistance with training and employment, but there is prior agreement with individuals on roles, rights and responsibilities. Residents are required to seek work or enter training and, with the help of staff, they draw up a self-development plan which is regularly reviewed. It is recognised, however, that these young people need time to develop confidence and life skills before they engage in education, and that initial progress can be slow.

Individuals can spend up to two years at the foyer, the average stay being around six months. One-quarter of the residents are aged 15 to 17 and most of the remainder are under 25. Two-thirds are male and one-third female. Up to one-third have been in trouble with the police. In the first two years of operation, 1,800 people went through the foyer programme, of whom 55 per cent found jobs and 18 per cent went into training.

The foyer movement has produced some good practice guides – one on working with TECs and one on working with social services. Another is being produced on working with colleges (Audit Commission, 1996; Williams, 1997b).

St Mungo's, a charity for the homeless, offers computer training for homeless people at Bridge House Centre near Westbourne Grove, as a way of helping them into education, training and jobs. Individuals are under no compulsion to attend and can learn at their own pace. The Charity has also run a computer scheme at its Christmas shelters – introducing people to e-mail, the Internet and sending CVs online. Those who took advantage of the facility benefited in a number of ways. According to a trainer: 'One group of young men were into all sorts of unmentionables. Learning about computers got them hooked. Their conversation changed from gambling and drugs to disk drives and operating systems. It was bizarre! What was unobtainable suddenly becomes accessible and you can see immediate results. It helps them rebuild confidence and self-esteem.'

Bridge House Centre is now developing links with local colleges and Welfare to Work schemes and will pay course fees if it is felt that they are appropriate and at the right level for the individuals concerned. Some young people have already been offered college places. A partnership has also been formed with Focus TEC: the TEC pays an allowance for homeless people who undertake NVQ training and also provides training for St Mungo's staff so that the Centre can offer NVQ training.

Young offenders

It is estimated that only about three per cent of young offenders nationally are involved in education or training, although up to 50 per cent of them have problems with reading, writing and maths. This could be one of the main barriers they face in finding employment and often leads to re-offending. Although it is the responsibility of probation services to advise individuals under their supervision on education, training and employment, and make appropriate referrals, there can be significant differences between services and individual officers in the extent of the information and help they provide. There is, however, greater recognition than there used to be of the link between poor educational attainment, unemployment and crime. Following the introduction of a core curriculum in prisons in 1996, the Home Office has funded probation offices around the country to pilot basic skills work with ex-offenders in collaboration with basic skills providers (Barnard 1998a). Additionally, Welfare to Work has been extended to 2,000 young prisoners in 11 prisons, in a 12-month pilot scheme which started in April 1998. This involves an 8-week course for inmates aged 18-24 nearing the end of their sentences. The programme incorporates in-depth assessment, basic and key skills and preparation for work courses. On release, individuals are also helped to find work opportunities or further study in their home areas (Travis, 1998).

Lancaster Farms Young Offenders' Institute provides inmates with training and support in a rural complex. All prisoners are entitled to at least five half days' education a week and can earn up to 10 for good behaviour. Those under 16 must receive at least 15 hours a week by law. The young men are offered education programmes provided by Lancaster and Morecambe College. These range from basic skills to A levels and include vocational training as well as courses in life skills, cooking, job-hunting and parenthood. All students are encouraged to work towards qualifications.

Since 1995, the prison has had a link with the YMCA to help the young men both before and after release. YMCA workers run a club two nights a week in the prison, offering advice workshops and training in personal and key skills such as team-working and leadership. The workers try and help the young men address their offending behaviour and provide them with coping strategies. They also link them up with their local YMCA association on release, help them to find accommodation and voluntary work and encourage employers to take them on.

Lancaster Farms also has an extensive peer education programme in which inmates are trained to support and advise others. Those who have participated in the peer counselling scheme are placed in cells with youngsters who are suspected of being suicidal (Spencer, 1997).

CHAPTER FIVE

Men over 25:
examples of approaches to
improve motivation and
participation

While there is a range of education and training initiatives targeted at young men and 'women returners', there appear to be comparatively few specifically targeted at men over 25. As long as men continue to dominate academic and vocational programmes in traditional male curriculum areas this presumably has not been seen as a priority. According to a college development worker: *'No-one really cares about low paid manual workers or men between their late 20s and 50s'.* Yet, as pointed out in Chapter 4, many men experience difficulty at key transition points in their lives and education could help them to manage these stages. Some adult education providers worry that they are not doing enough to cater specifically for men but those who do organise programmes for specific male groups often find it difficult to recruit sufficient numbers to make a course viable.

Recruitment issues

Information and advice
Men often claim that they are not aware of the range of adult education and training opportunities available. This could be partly because they have limited sources of information. Both the 1997 National Adult Learning Survey and the 1996 NIACE/Gallup adult learning survey confirmed that, whereas women obtain information from a wide range of sources such as friends, family, education providers, TV and newspapers, the most common source of information on learning opportunities for men is their employer (Table 36, see p130). For unemployed men, the main source of information about learning opportunities is also usually a work-related environment such as Benefit Offices, or Job Clubs.

Sometimes it is the language used in publicity that is the problem. Non-specific course titles may fail to stimulate interest while acronyms, educational jargon and references to assessment may have a deterrent effect.

Although conventional publicity often fails to attract men to adult education and training programmes, many do respond to information provided in other ways. According to some practitioners, an effective recruitment method is to enlist the help of female partners. This has been found particularly effective with older, retired men, many of whom tend to rely on their wives for social contacts and activities outside the home.

Another recommended recruitment method is for existing male learners to act as 'ambassadors' informing men from a similar social background about the learning opportunities available and the potential benefits. This has been found to be particularly effective with male manual workers.

Telephone 'helplines'

Men also seem to respond to information provided over the telephone:

During the annual **NIACE-led Adult Learners' Week**, a free telephone hotline provides information and advice on learning opportunities. In the fortnight leading up to the week, information about the helpline is enclosed in the envelope in which unemployed people receive their Girocheques. As a result, more than half of the people telephoning the helpline have been long-term unemployed people, many of them men, seeking information and advice on education, training and careers. About 40 per cent of enquirers have subsequently joined an education or training course (Sargant *et al*, 1997).

Careers on Call, a confidential telephone helpline funded by FOCUS, the central London Training and Enterprise Council, provides free information and advice on careers, education, training and qualifications, for people living or working in the London boroughs of Camden, City of London, Hackney, Hammersmith and Fulham, Islington, Kensington and Chelsea, Lambeth, Southwark and the City of Westminster. The helpline started in January 1997. It was advertised on bus tickets and local radio and people were referred to it by the Employment Services, the Careers Service, Job Clubs, TECs, libraries and education and training providers.

In the first month of operation, there were 650 enquiries; in the sixth, 1,800. Sixty per cent of callers were male and over 50 per cent aged 26-39. Sixty per cent were unemployed and 40 per cent black and from other non-white communities.

As well as referring callers to education and training providers, advice agencies and funding providers, the service mails out information. It also produces a monthly vacancy list for government training schemes in the central London area (Women Returners Network, 1997).

These examples suggest that the new national helpline, Learning Direct, launched in February 1998 at the time of the Green Paper on lifelong learning, will be a potentially valuable source of information for men. The helpline received over 3,000 calls in its first days of operation. These came from equal numbers of both men and women, mostly aged between 26 and 45. Thirty-nine per cent were enquiring about further and higher education, 20 per cent about training, 10 per cent about careers information and 10 per cent about training in information technology (Crequer, 1998).

Guidance in informal settings

Male non-participants will also respond to face-to-face provision of information and guidance when delivered in a sensitive and appropriate way in familiar locations in which they feel comfortable and at ease.

Joint finance from the local education authority and health authority for a **primary health care scheme in Gloucester** enabled an educational guidance worker to provide a weekly service at five local health practices. In each participating surgery, information on local education opportunities was provided in the waiting room and a room was made available for private interviews. People were referred to the guidance worker by doctors, health visitors, practice nurses, receptionists, community nurses and psychiatric nurses. These were fully briefed about the scheme at the start of a practice's participation. Referrals were at their discretion but certain groups were particularly targeted: long-term unemployed people, people with long-term health or disability problems, people who were depressed, stressed or low in self-esteem, elderly or isolated individuals, single parents and people with minor mental health problems.

Individuals who were referred could book a private interview with the guidance worker who would discuss with them their interests and provide information and advice on appropriate education or training routes in the Gloucester area.

The scheme proved very successful in helping and encouraging – among other groups – men with poor basic skills and unemployed middle-aged men on disability allowance, to take up local educational opportunities with very beneficial results. Evaluations of the impact of the scheme indicated that few of the people helped were previously aware of the local learning opportunities available or that these opportunities were open to them. Moreover, the majority of respondents admitted that they would not have had the confidence to approach an education or training provider for information before speaking to the guidance worker.

The location of the service was one of the keys to its effectiveness. Many participants stated that the doctor's surgery was a familiar environment in which they felt comfortable. Another key factor was the appointment of a guidance worker with the skills and sensitivity to put people at their ease, listen to them and make appropriate and constructive suggestions. The words 'encouragement', 'hope', 'motivation', 'sympathy' and 'understanding' were frequently used by participants to describe their impression of the initial interview (McGivney, 1997).

Outreach strategies

Reaching non-participant men can be time-intensive. As the last example illustrates, it requires one-to-one contact and dialogue in familiar local venues. Imaginative outreach strategies are needed for those who are geographically and socially isolated. *'The trick is to bring learning to learners wherever they are, whether it be in family rooms in primary schools, libraries, betting shops, snooker halls, rooms above pubs, or shopping malls. Adult learners often prefer to study alongside their peers.'* (Kennedy, 1997: 8)

Some groups of men can be drawn into learning through their interest in sport.

Alive and Kicking, a project funded by the Department of Health, used Sunday football as a method of addressing men's health issues and encouraging greater health awareness among men. In the West Midlands, where over 35,000 men play Sunday football, two Sunday leagues participated in the project. Individual players in the clubs which registered with the project completed health awareness activities. In return the clubs received points leading to prizes such as first aid kits, match balls and a full team kit for the outright winner. Twelve clubs participated and over 200 men took part (CEDC, 1997).

Pubs, another largely male preserve, are being increasingly used as a venue for informal education activities.

Building on the growing interest in quiz night sessions, **Airedale and Wharfedale College** has organised short, accredited courses and discussion groups in local pubs.

With funding from the European Year of Lifelong Learning, **Inn-Tuition**, a programme of pub-based learning modules, was initiated by a Leeds further education college in partnership with a local brewery,

Local shopping malls are also being increasingly used as an effective first contact point.

The Learning World is situated in Gateshead Metro Centre, the largest retail mall in Europe. It was set up by Gateshead College and Sunderland University in 1996 and provides drop-in learning centres offering information and advice on education and careers as well as courses ranging from information technology to degree level programmes. Over 4,000 people have taken advantage of the service since the Learning World was launched (Hackett, 1998).

Responsive approaches

Former non-participants who return to learning often do so not because they have been attracted by a leaflet or brochure but because they have been approached in a way that chimes with their current interests and concerns, for example, interest in the environment, lack of amenities, local housing issues – none of which are necessarily perceived as learning needs – but which sensitive outreach workers have responded to with a learning response. This approach has set many individuals on a learning path.

The Coalfields Learning Project in Yorkshire offers a confidential advice and guidance service, community group skills training and courses in different subjects and at various levels, in response to expressed needs and interests. Activities are organised in places and at times that suit learners. The project also provides information about, and organises group visits to, Northern College and other organisations offering learning opportunities.

The project is characterised by intensive outreach development work, community-based activities, responsiveness to identified needs and partnership with the local community based on trust. There is a bespoke curriculum but the community base is linked to progression routes.

Organisers have found that older men – aged 45-60 – are the most likely male recruits and they are interested in hobby/interest-related courses, community volunteering and capacity-building. (Stephen Brunt, presentation to NIACE Annual Study Conference 1998)

A development worker at a college in the south of England has been using local authority funding to stimulate interest in further education among low skilled and unskilled men, former service men and homeless people. He visits his local pub – 'a traditional working-class boozer' – and talks to regulars about the opportunities the college might offer them. He is assisted in this by a local man, a welder in a local firm, who also works part-time at the pub and is someone who is known and trusted by local people. He has now been seconded by his firm for one day a week to assist with the project. This approach has resulted in a successful series of computer workshops at the pub, as well as drop-in information events on engineering skills. *'It takes hard footwork and chatting people up. But when men get to know you and trust you, they talk to you and start telling you the kinds of things they'd like to do.'*

The development worker has experienced no problem in arousing interest among men; the difficult bit has been to galvanise the college to respond in an appropriate manner: *'It's not flexible enough – it's big and bureaucratic and things move very slowly; some staff are patronising and negative. FEFC finding is not flexible enough. The men want short courses – six weeks – in things like basic skills. It is crackable but I have to protect them from snotty colleagues.'*

Local research into attitudes and needs

Lack of responsiveness by education institutions to the needs of people who do not traditionally engage in learning has long been a formidable obstacle to working class participation. However, the recent succession of policy reports and initiatives to encourage lifelong learning and widen participation have prompted a new concern to meet the needs of all adult learners rather than those who are easiest to recruit. One way of doing this is through research. Research into non-participant attitudes and needs can inform recruitment and admissions practices and identify what changes should be made to the curriculum and learning environment.

A study of men's participation in further education was conducted in North Yorkshire, funded by **North Yorkshire TEC**. It involved all the further education and sixth form colleges in the TEC region and included surveys, interviews and focus groups involving over 1,000 men, both participants and non-participants. This approach enabled researchers to identify the groups that were hardest to attract and institutions were subsequently given a small sum of money from the TEC's FE development fund to target these groups. The resulting activities included taster days in pubs and working men's clubs, a pub quiz, pilot courses, and collaboration with a football club in the dissemination of publicity and promotional events. In one college, male students were invited to compile a prospectus aimed specifically at men and others acted as college 'ambassadors', promoting taster events and college provision among their male peers.

A further proposed strategy is to investigate the gender composition of college admissions and information staff. (Carolyn Stoakes, presentation at the NIACE Annual Study Conference, 1998)

Collective approaches

Since peer group norms are particularly strong among men, group approaches through workplaces and community organisations are often more effective than the targeting of individuals.

Employee development schemes which are open to the whole workforce and offer financial support for learning opportunities, have been remarkably effective in attracting men at all occupational levels to non-work-related education. One of the best known employee development schemes, the **Ford Employee Development and Assistance Programme** (EDAP,) attracted 20,000, mainly male, manual employees in its first year of operation. Forty-two per cent of manual workers in the assembly plant at Dagenham participated in courses of various kind through EDAP over a three-year period – more than double the rate of participation in education for this section of the population as a whole. More than half of these employees were engaging in formal education for the first time since they left school. Although some of them had considered enrolling in courses before, they had lacked the motivation or courage to follow up the idea (Beattie, 1997).

A number of factors account for the effectiveness of employee development schemes, notably the provision of financial help, on-site information and guidance, and organisation of learning opportunities at times which suit shift workers, making it possible for them to attend courses with their peers in a familiar working environment. However, a key element in the success of the employee development model is the offer of opportunities to all workers rather than to specific groups which means that participation comes to be regarded as normal rather than exceptional: *'If non-participation is seen to be the norm, participation is unlikely to increase. Publicity [about the EDAP scheme] is therefore given to the fact that a large and growing number of employees already participate.'* (Beattie, 1997: 17)

Another factor that accounts for the effectiveness of employee development schemes is that they are not imposed by management but often originate as a partnership between employers and the workforce or their union representatives.

Help with costs

Worries about financial costs deter people of both sexes from engaging in learning. As employee development schemes have shown, the provision of small amounts of financial assistance for learning can have a powerful motivational effect among people in lower income groups.

In Birmingham there is a **Weekend College** scheme in which further education institutions and other providers stay open at the weekends to provide training for individuals who wish to improve their skills. The TEC provides vouchers which give holders access to educational and careers guidance and to courses run at weekends by colleges and other accredited providers. The training is for up to 16 hours, spread over several weekends. About 2,000 people attend the courses each year. Many are employed people wishing to improve their skills. Forty-five per cent subsequently progress to other training or education courses which they fund themselves.

The scheme has proved so successful that it has been extended to local businesses so that employers can send their staff for training at weekends. This has proved particularly attractive to small organisations which cannot manage without employees during the working week (NACETT, 1997a).

To encourage people to engage in education or training, **Kent TEC** has offered individuals vouchers worth £50 which can be exchanged for information and advice on education, training and careers (TES, 30 May 1997).

Designing programmes for men

Post compulsory education providers often offer programmes to help women develop themselves and plan for the future but there are comparatively few similar courses targeted specifically at men (although some might say there is no apparent demand for these). In view of the numbers of unemployed and insecurely employed men, this seems short-sighted:

'The response of the adult education service, apart from its involvement in TEC-sponsored training initiatives has been limited in its reaction to the work needs of unemployed men.' (Neville, 1994: 208)

Some adult education providers, however, have recognised that the lack of programmes designed for men is a gap which needs to be addressed.

As noted in Chapter 2, however, men are harder to reach than women and one of the biggest obstacles to men's participation is anxiety about status and losing face. In all-male groups they do not feel so exposed. According to a tutor in computer skills, participants like learning with other men: *because of the mutual support they provide each other. They also feel more comfortable in a single sex group as they believe women have better keyboard skills.'*

It is important, therefore, that learning activities directed at non-participant groups do not imply a skills or knowledge deficiency but validate existing knowledge and skills.

The London Borough of Waltham Forest Adult Education Service offers courses exclusively targeted at men. The borough has a large (30 per cent) minority ethnic population, higher than average male unemployment and high levels of under-achievement and exclusion among boys at school. The new courses include:

Back to the Grindstone? A 60-hour preparation for return to work or study for older men including individual educational, occupational guidance interview with a personal action plan and psychometric testing; basic skills training; tasters of other subjects; job search and interview techniques.

Working with Kids – it's a Man's Job! A course designed to offer a first step in training for work with children as crèche worker, after-school-club playcare worker, nursery or play group worker. Participants can progress to NVQ courses in playwork or childcare or go directly into employment. (The adult education service already has male crèche workers and can offer part-time employment opportunities. It is also expected that expansion of after-school provision will create a need for trained staff.)

Introduction to Computers for Dads and Lads: a course in which fathers learn about computers with their sons.

Family learning

Most family learning programmes are attended exclusively by women although men have a range of talents and resources that could contribute towards children's educational progress. Recognition of this led coordinators of **Bristol Community Education** to devise a family learning programme specifically for men. This gained financial support from the Extending Learning Communities Award scheme administered by NIACE.

A steering group for the project was set up, composed of representatives from local organisations including schools and the University of the West of England. The initial tasks of the group were to arrange for research to be conducted in a working-class area where men had limited access to adult education opportunities and to organise some pilot family learning taster sessions for men.

A local man, a father who was already helping at the local nursery school, was appointed as development worker. He conducted a small survey involving personal letters and follow-up interviews among male parents or carers of pupils at a local primary school. Responses indicated that a majority of men were already helping their children with their education and that most would be interested in helping at their children's local school or nursery. In keeping with other evidence, the men expressed most interest in practical learning activities to do with computers, motor mechanics, carpentry, bricklaying, sports and electronics.

On the basis of this feedback, three family learning taster events were held in bricklaying, computing and woodwork. These were held at the local school at different times to enable men and children to work in small groups together on joint activities. It was hoped that this would not only increase the men's own confidence but would also provide male pupils with positive male role models. A school teacher led the computer session while the bricklaying and woodwork sessions were led by male tutors from the local community.

Twenty-five men participated in the sessions over three days. Reactions were very positive and the experience of working with children was considered both enjoyable and effective. The majority were interested in continuing learning either with children or in adult part-time courses. Thus the taster session acted as an effective route into education for men previously uninvolved in family or adult learning.

The success of the scheme has been attributed to two key factors: the employment of a local development worker experienced in helping in early education settings, who used a personal approach and was able to win the trust and interest of other local men; and the basing of learning activities on men's existing skills rather than using an approach that implied a skills deficiency. (Source: Jane Taylor, Bristol Community Education Service.)

A male-centred approach

Programmes that are offered to men are often based on a model that has been successfully used with women. However, the kind of programmes that attract women, do not necessarily appeal to men as the following example demonstrates.

In 1996, the **Women's Access Project in East Leicestershire and Rutland**, which operates from local colleges and community education centres, initiated some courses for men, using methods that had proved effective in Return to Learn courses for women. However, workers soon discovered that men were harder to reach than women and the scale of demand for education was smaller. Conventional publicity did not work and recruitment was better achieved by door-knocking and word of mouth via the women attending women's courses.

The curriculum also had to be rethought. At first coordinators tried offering a broad programme like the one offered to women, incorporating personal development and vocational skills. However it, was found that men had a narrower field of interest and were less interested in personal development. The most popular area for men seemed to be IT so the project concentrated on this as a starting point and potential pathway into other subject areas.

The programme now offers Open College Network-accredited Introduction to Computing level 2 and all students complete a national Record of Achievement. Sessions also include careers advice with individuals and small groups. The need to offer support in basic skills, particularly literacy, was rapidly identified and this has been integrated into the programme. For those who wish to continue learning, there are progression routes to further education.

The course is offered weekly and is free for men who are on state benefits while those in paid employment can pay on a sessional basis. It used to be run in the morning or early afternoon but this had to be changed to 4.30pm to suit the school where the computer room is located. The course has been offered to 14 men at a time (to match the number of available computers) although the number dropped when the timing was changed. Participants have included unemployed men, men on disability allowance, older men and those who have been made redundant or taken early retirement. There are also some employed men. Most are aged from the late 30s upwards. (Information supplied by Katie Clarricoates, Community Tutor and Warden Belvoir High School and Community Centre.)

The coordinator of the initiative described above has found that women tend to be at a similar stage when they return to learning and have a core of interests in common. They respond to general programmes with a varied content and a focus on self-development. Men tend to have fewer shared characteristics and a narrower range of learning interests. Some of the feelings they have, however, such as lack of confidence and a sense of being under-valued (especially if they are unemployed) are broadly the same as those experienced by women. She has found that just getting men involved in a learning programme, whatever the subject, can, as for women, help them develop confidence and motivation, but to attract men in the first place, courses need to have a specific focus and clear, self-explanatory titles. Others have reported similar findings. Neville (1994) has described how a course for men which was advertised under '*the rather vague title New Directions for Men*' attracted only three men. When the title was made more explicit – *Careers Guidance for Men* – there were 17 enquiries and 11 men subsequently enrolled. The course is described below:

A 10-week course entitled **Changing Course – Careers Guidance for Men**, organised by the University of Bradford Access initiative, was mounted at a local community centre. It attracted 11 participants, more than half of whom were from a semi- or unskilled work background. The tutor was male and the course focused on issues relevant to group members – employment, state benefits, ageism and the costs of education. After a 'wary' start, the group quickly '*bonded together and with the* *tutor'*. Two men left after the third week having found out all they wanted to know and another two left halfway through the course to take up jobs. The remainder stayed till the end and three men from working-class backgrounds applied to a local college to do full-time courses. The others decided to stay in part-time general and vocational education while continuing to sign on (Neville, 1994).

Practical programmes

A further education development worker who has been trying to increase the participation of men in the south of England has found that they are initially attracted by focused, single-interest, practical activities but that, once they have become involved in learning, they often move on to other things: *'Mostly they start with vocational stuff and then turn to non-vocational, the opposite of what is usually thought.'*

Men usually participate in learning for practical and job-related reasons. This is true regardless of whether they are unemployed or in work. For many men, especially those in low income groups, learning is an activity undertaken only when it is relevant to their everyday life and concerns: *'My candid feeling is that if someone's on a very low income then they're ducking and diving, trying to get self-employment. If they take time off to learn it costs them opportunity time. They tend to see education and training as a way of making money or making life more interesting. They want things to help them with their jobs.'* (FE development worker)

The study of men and further education conducted in North Yorkshire (North Yorkshire TEC, 1997) indicated that both those who were learning and those who were not viewed education in later life primarily as a way to improve job prospects, improve current work performance and increase job security. Respondents of all ages wanted participation in further education to lead to tangible benefits such as jobs or increased pay and status in the workplace.

National and regional surveys regularly produce similar findings. Male respondents to the National Adult Learning Survey (SCPR, 1997) were considerably more likely than female respondents to say that they might participate in learning if there were employment benefits. Similarly, a survey of men attending Access courses in West Yorkshire (Neville, 1996) revealed that their main reason for participating was work-related although the course provided some with an escape route from unsatisfactory employment or unemployment.

Programmes targeted at men need to respond to this instrumental orientation and particularly their interest in work. Programmes that set out to appeal to other motives, for example, social contacts and interaction, are more likely to attract women than men. In his study of voluntary organisations, Elsdon (1995) found men less willing than women to recognise and admit social motives in joining voluntary groups and far less likely to admit the value and satisfaction of social interaction even in groups where these were of paramount importance (for example, those based on cooperation and teamwork).

Information and communication technology (ICT)

Some providers have found that the best way of attracting men is to provide courses in ICT. Many men find computer-based learning less threatening than a group situation. According to an adult education development worker: *'Men hate admitting that they are wrong and IT helps to hide their inadequacies.'*

Open Learning Credits, an open learning programme for unemployed people piloted by TECs, attracted male groups who rarely participated in Training for Work: older men made redundant after 20-30 years in a job and unemployed middle managers. These were apparently attracted by the 'safe' learning method in which their performance was not exposed to the view of others. Although the programme was popular and successful, it was withdrawn ostensibly because of difficulties in changing the rules of Training for Work to accommodate Open Learning.

It has also been found that the Internet is a potentially important means of engaging men in learning. The majority of users are men, many of whom join mail groups in specific interest areas such as gardening, stamp collecting and sports.

Although men are more likely than women to use the new technologies, research evidence suggests that access varies enormously between different geographical areas and neighbourhoods as well as between different socio-economic and age groups. Older people, poor and unskilled groups and those living in rural or inner-city areas are the least likely to have access to computers. For this reason, IBM and the Community Development Foundation have established a national working party on Social Inclusion in the Information Society to examine the impact of new information technologies on local communities. The aim is to investigate how new technology can help society to be more socially inclusive. A range of projects have been sponsored for this purpose (Midgley, 1997c).

With support from the Extending Learning Communities fund, the London Borough of Waltham Forest Adult Education Service has run two courses entitled **Introduction to Computers for Dads and Sons**. Publicity, which was concentrated in estates in areas with high levels of deprivation, generated 60 enquires. The courses were held on Saturdays for 10 participants at a time, five adults and five children (aged 7 to 13) . A registration fee of £6 per family was charged. The courses were taught by male tutors who found teaching two generations a challenge, particularly as sons were sometimes more experienced in computer use than their fathers, and they needed to choose software and develop a teaching methodology that appealed to both age groups. The initiative was considered a great success. The opportunity to learn with their sons on

Saturdays attracted men's participation. As a result of the experience, the adult education service is considering offering other courses for family groups. (Information supplied by Mary Crowley, Waltham Forest Adult Education service.)

Men's discussion groups and development courses

Education and training courses for women often offer participants an opportunity to reflect on their experience and situation as women in society. It is far less common for men involved in an education programme to reflect together on what it means to be a man in the modern world.

As outlined in Chapter 3, men's roles and relationships to work and family have undergone considerable changes in recent years, and many of the old certainties have disappeared. Male discussion groups can help men to explore their fears, attitudes and experience with other men in a safe environment. Topics that might usefully be covered are:

- Gender roles: how these are socially constructed and evolving; socialisation and conditioning; traditional notions of masculinity and their effect on male behaviour.
- Diversity and difference: the power of male, female and racial stereotypes: '*it is a luxury not to have to think about race or class or gender. (...) Only those marginalised by some category understand how powerful that category is when deployed against them.*' (Kimmel, 1996: 45).
- Male violence and dealing with conflict.
- Men's changing relationship to work and the labour market.
- Men's family role, especially as parents. (Changing social and work patterns offer men the opportunity to become more involved parents. Will they grasp it?)
- Health issues (diet, drinking, smoking, exercise, safe sex).
- Relationships with others; communication; expressing feelings and emotion.

Some consider the latter topic a particularly important one:

'*If men could feel and express their feelings particularly grief and fear it would make adjustment to a new role much easier. It would reduce the chances of men's anger leading to self-victimising and women-blaming. It would also improve their physical and mental health, their relationships with partners and children, and have a big impact on their propensity for violence (...). The increasing level of crises in men's lives (especially in relation to work and relationships) is inevitably bringing them into greater contact with their emotions − even the stiffest of upper lips can quiver when faced with redundancy or divorce. Moreover, we all now live in a culture in which therapy-speak is ever more widespread and emotional expression increasingly validated. But most men still need to go much further before they can finally shake off the claim that they are actually little more emotional than a robot encased in bubble-wrap.'* (Baker, 1996: 33-34)

The Friends Meeting House in Cambridge is holding a **'Saturday Blokes Day'**. This will be: *'a day of discussion and inspiration for men and guys brave enough to attend a confidential group setting out to discuss old fashioned stereotypes and new ideas. We want to talk about thoughts and feelings instead of doing what men do a lot when they get together – talk generalities and leave out the personal. Men don't feel safe talking about these things.'* (Millard, 1998)

The Wales National Health Service Equality Unit has established a men's development course involving 6 one-day workshops and two residential, 24-hour sessions. This allows men to discuss in safety and confidence many of the issues that concern them as men in today's society.

Programmes of this type often have difficulty recruiting as many men feel that discussion of personal matters is either irrelevant or threatening. Men-only groups also require leaders and tutors with considerable sensitivity and skills.

Tutor skills

The inclusion of gender issues is not yet a priority in staff training and is often considered a matter that just concerns women. Yet, given many of the problems men face (and cause) in society, training programmes for people working with men could usefully incorporate an emphasis on understanding male conditioning and concepts of masculinity:

'There is surprisingly little understanding of men and masculinity among those whose job it is to work with men in a context where gender is acutely relevant – this certainly includes police officers, probation and prison officers, social workers, health care professionals and teachers. Given the rapidly changing context of men's lives, and the fact that men constitute the most problematic group now dealt with by many agencies, it is more important than ever for all those working with men to have an understanding of their issues. But, when gender is addressed in professional training programmes, it is normally as an option and concerned solely with women, rather than incorporating a critical understanding of masculinity. This seems outdated and unworkable, perhaps most obviously in the case of violent men, for whom the traditional – and obviously largely useless – response is imprisonment combined with neglect. A greater understanding of the psychological roots of violent behaviour, intertwined as they are with masculinity, would create the opportunity for a more creative, and more effective, approach.' (Baker, 1996: 39)

Teaching and learning approaches

Tutors working with men find that the informal teaching styles preferred by many women are often resisted. Some men feel threatened or embarrassed by small group or paired work which requires an element of self-disclosure. It has been found that men often prefer a more didactic, whole group approach and practical, activity-based learning. A tutor working with adult male students has found that he needs:

> 'to work with men's vulnerability and insecurity about being found out for "not knowing" – and even conceal what you're doing if necessary. They can escape from their insecurity by being involved in activity. If learning can be cleverly stitched into activities such as computers or sport without their being conscious of it, it can be effective although this requires cleverness and skill'.

Is single sex provision legal?

Training   The Sex Discrimination Act (SDA) allows for provision, on the same terms, for either women or men. Section 47 of the Act 1975, which allowed for single sex provision under certain circumstances was modified in 1986. The three conditions under which it was legal to provide single sex training remained the same. Single sex provision can be offered in cases where it appears that in the preceding 12 months particular work has been carried out solely or mainly by one sex in an area within Great Britain. It can also be offered in order to train for employment those who have not been in regular full-time employment for a time because of domestic or family responsibilities. Training can include courses to develop confidence and the basic skills necessary for a return to employment or further training; courses which involve job sampling or work experience; compensatory courses in specific subjects; guidance or counselling for people returning to work.

Other types of provision   Section 29 of the Act deals with the provision of goods, facilities, services and leisure provision . Under this section, those providing goods, facilities or services which are designed for one sex are not required to provide the corresponding goods, services or facilities designed for the other sex. This applies also to skills which may be exercised in a different way for men and women (for example, hairdressing). The section also allows facilities and services to be restricted to one sex if they are such that users are likely to suffer 'serious embarrassment at the presence of the opposite sex'. Single sex discussion groups of the kind discussed above would be covered under these provisions.

Workplace learning

The experience of employee development schemes in recent years provides ample evidence that men will participate in both work-related and non-work-related learning when flexible opportunities are provided through the workplace. The evidence also shows, however, that the majority of employers concentrate training on their younger, more qualified and higher grade workers, and many workplaces do not encourage independent learning by providing information on the educational opportunities available to adults. One of the most effective ways of engaging men in learning would therefore be by persuading employers to train or retrain their manual, lower skilled and older workers. There are sound economic reasons for doing this. *The Employment in Europe 1996* report (EC, 1996) argues that updating the skills of older workers and upgrading and broadening the skills of lower skilled workers while in work, could be the most significant and cost-effective investment in preventing long-term unemployment and increasing employability.

Trade unions

Research evidence indicates that employees working in unionised workplaces are twice as likely to be trained as those in workplaces where unions are not recognised, and that managers who share decision-making over skills acquisition are the most successful in transforming workforce attitudes to training and change (Perman, 1998:26).

Unions have an important role in helping lower-skilled men acquire education, training and qualifications. They can provide education and training for their members as well as negotiate with employers for provision of learning opportunities. Union representatives can also act as educational guidance workers. There are union education programmes which train members to act as effective representatives and to advise their work-mates on appropriate learning pathways (Perman, 1998).

The Trades Union Congress (TUC) Education Service delivers training for an estimated 30,000 representatives a year on day release and short courses. Accreditation is provided by the National Open College Network (NOCN) for trade union officers through the TUC National Education Centre.

The TUC has been running 10 **Bargaining for Skills projects** with 60 Training and Enterprise Councils (TECs) in England and Wales. The projects involve collaboration between unions and employers in creating employee awareness of education and training opportunities. Training courses are also provided through the TUC Education Service. These help representatives to understand different training initiatives and develop the skills to negotiate for learning opportunities (Perman, 1998).

Management and trade unionists at **Tinsley Park Mill**, owned by British Steel Engineering Steels, have been running a free voluntary education programme jointly funded for the first two years by British Steel and Sheffield TEC. After work, employees can follow a range of accredited and non-accredited courses in areas such as foreign languages, computing, computer-aided design, stained-glass making, acoustic guitar, painting, Tai Chi, motor mechanics, clay modelling, wood carving and brickwork.

One of the main education providers, Sheffield College, enrols students on site at Tinsley Park Mill. This has proved an effective recruitment strategy for former non-learners. According to one: 'Walking through college doors would have been a very big step for people who have not been in education for a long time. Enrolling people on site together with their work-mates was a big plus.'

A 35-year-old production worker in the steel industry who was learning Spanish described his first reactions to the scheme: 'What's the firm going to get out of it? You don't get anything for nothing these days. I was also a bit wary. I used to think chaps who went to night classes were a bunch of anoraks. But there's a real mixed bunch in my class including policemen and footballers. I've really been enjoying myself. It gives me an opportunity to mix with people I wouldn't meet, so you also get a broader outlook.' (Hampshire, 1997)

Unemployed men

One of the most painful transitions for men is the loss of a job – something which the pace of industrial change has made increasingly common. The first priority of those affected, however, will not be learning, but work – the need for secure employment and restoration of the confidence, pride and status that loss of work has removed from them. Education or training can help towards these goals although many men will need to be convinced of this. One of the (numerous) problems in encouraging unemployed men to participate is that the link between unemployment and lack of education and qualifications is not always clear. Despite the assumption implicit in many programmes for long-term unemployed people, unemployment is not just a consequence of lack of basic or specific skills and lack of 'flexibility' on the part of individuals. It is also the consequence of changing global and domestic markets, domestic economic policies, industrial and organisational restructuring and rampant ageism in the labour market. Often it is the result of ill health and disability (McGivney, 1992a). Many unemployed men are highly trained, skilled and experienced workers who are not to blame for the restructuring, downsizing or overall scaling-down of industries that have destroyed their jobs. The implication that they are not sufficiently 'employable' can be insulting.

A number of new measures have been launched to assist unemployed adults back into work or training. The New Deal which is mainly targeted at people aged 18-24 has now been extended to people aged 25 plus who have been unemployed for 18 months or more. As noted in Chapter 2, most of these are men. Pilot programmes were launched in November 1998 for about 90,000 people. These will consist of two phases, each lasting three months. The first is an advisory process involving individual interviews, job search and training needs assessment. The second, described as 'mandatory activity', involves individually tailored help which might include job specific training, pre-vocational training, help into self-employment, work trials or work experience in the voluntary sector. From June 1998 there has been a weekly subsidy for employers who take on any of the over-25s who have been unemployed for two years or more. For the first time too there is special help for unemployed people aged over 50, with programmes *'expected to take account of their special circumstances and make the most of their existing skills and work experience.'* (Convery, 1998a)

To succeed in their objectives, the new initiatives may need to overcome initial scepticism. Government schemes for the unemployed are associated with the threat of sanctions (loss of state benefits) and there is a persisting suspicion that they may have more to do with reducing the size of the unemployment register than with helping people find secure employment. Those who have been unemployed for lengthy periods will want to see clear pay-offs from programmes in the form of enhanced job opportunities. Many former schemes have signally failed to demonstrate such outcomes. In the extraordinary succession of stop-start programmes for the unemployed since the 1980s, the most effective and popular were invariably those which were cut or curtailed – the former Training Access Points (TAPs) and Community Programme are cases in point. More recently, TEC training budgets have been cut, resulting in loss of some programmes. Despite evidence of their proven appeal to unemployed men, so many changes have been imposed on Business Start-Up programmes that it has become increasingly difficult for unemployed people to acquire information and help on starting their own business (Murray, 1998a).

It is vital that programmes for unemployed men, especially those who have been made redundant after working for many years, are not perceived to be punitive or based on insulting assumptions about their skills and lack of 'employability'. Those who formerly worked in traditional industries such as mining are highly skilled. Moreover there can be a chronic shortage of alternative jobs in the areas where male-dominated industries have been destroyed. If programmes for the unemployed do not take account of the harsh realities of the labour market, particularly in some of the most depressed industrial areas, they simply heighten feelings of depression, distrust and cynicism (McGivney, 1992a).

People dealing with the unemployed also need to take account of their individual situation. Career action plans, for example, may not have much relevance for older men or unemployed manual workers who have to deal on a day-to-day basis with an uncertain and casual labour market and very insecure finances. However, *'One of the problems is attitudes of benefit centres. They're so unsympathetic, and blokes are getting into long-term debt problems.'* (FE lecturer)

According to Banks and Davies (1990), any strategy to increase the motivation of unemployed people needs: *'to take account of what they themselves want, what they believe they can achieve and the kind of risks and costs they are prepared to accommodate.'* It is often argued that long-term unemployed men do not need a succession of training schemes; they need *real* work experience.

Glasgow Works is an example of what is described as the intermediate labour market approach to reducing long-term unemployment. The idea is to increase people's employability by offering them real work experience. The scheme offers up to a year of paid work with additional training and personal support in local regeneration projects delivered through local partnerships between the public, private and voluntary sectors.

The programme is targeted at people who have been unemployed for over a year, and 40 per cent of participants have been jobless for more than two years.

Between 1994 and spring 1997, over 800 people passed through the programme. In the autumn of 1996, 62 per cent of all leavers had found a job. The success of the Scottish model is attributed to the fact that participants earn a wage while learning new skills which are of practical benefit to the local community and economy. The scheme has influenced new measures for the unemployed in England, including Neighbourhood Match and aspects of the New Deal (Marshall, 1997; Murray, 1998b).

Support for unemployed men

Unemployed men who participate in training may require all or some of the following: sympathetic careers guidance, personal counselling, confidence-building exercises, job search skills, practical help with developing a range of skills, financial and debt counselling, and practical work experience.

The Link Project based in Tower Hamlets supports local unemployed people by offering a comprehensive service which includes vocational advice and guidance, personal development, motivation and orientation; language and basic skills support, job search, guided CV writing, interview skills training and analysis, and feedback on unsuccessful interviews. All processes focus on helping users find successful routes into learning or work.

Ninety per cent of users of the project are from minority ethnic groups including 70 per cent Bangladeshi, 10 per cent Somali and 8 per cent other black and Asian groups.

The project is funded by the Employment Service, the London East TEC's Passport Initiative and the European Social Fund. It is housed in the Bethnal Green Training Centre, an informal environment where staff reflect the ethnic and cultural profile of the area. There is a worker seconded from the local Job Centre who provides information on Employment Service provision and entitlements. Access is available on a drop-in basis and users can return as often as they need for ongoing support and guidance. The project is linked to Tower Hamlets Summer University and through systematic outreach work with local youth groups, young people are referred to the project for support and advice (NICEC, 1998).

Preparatory training

Some long-term unemployed people are not ready to enter formal training schemes. To deal with their requirements, special preparatory programmes have been piloted by TECs.

In 1996-97, **pre-vocational pilots** were run by TECs for unemployed people needing help with basic, social and life skills before they could successfully take part in employment or training programmes. The 11,000 participants included ex-offenders, people with disabilities and those with English as their second language. The pilots were subsequently integrated into the Training for Work programme for about 30,000 people.

The programmes were between 12 and 30 weeks long and covered vocational skills, qualifications and progression, and personal and social development. They included in-depth, one-to-one support and a focus on self-help and peer support.

Evaluation revealed that the combination of ongoing assessment, vocational training and work experience with advice, guidance and personal support was successful in supporting both vocational and personal progression. The pilots enabled participants to move into Training for Work and other Employment Service programmes and, in some cases, to find work or supported employment. One of the most important outcomes identified was that individual's confidence and motivation were considerably increased.

The pilots involved partnerships and networking between TECs, the Employment Service and training providers with expertise in working with the client groups. The evaluators recommend that future programmes should also involve organisations with expertise in housing and health needs. Quality assurance procedures should also be extended to include follow-up of clients who fail to complete their programme (Dewson *et al*, 1997).

Informal networking

Many unemployed people acquire contacts and jobs through their informal networks of friends, former colleagues and acquaintances. However, the services and programmes designed for unemployed people cater exclusively for individuals who are all in the same situation. Perri6 and Lawson (1996) maintain that programmes which isolate unemployed people will fail: what is needed is a new approach to counteract their 'network poverty' by enabling them to mix with a range of people:

'Unemployed people need a wider range of weak ties with as many people as possible rather than a comfort blanket of strong ties with people in exactly the same position as themselves. The welfare state actively damages the chances of unemployed people by creating this kind of social network. It locks people into network poverty (...) It means an end to testing whether claimants are actively seeking work by the number of pointless letters they write. Instead, claimants should be asked who they've asked about jobs, where they've put the word out and what they can do to broaden their social networks. Research conducted at the London School of Economics found that the chances of someone finding a job

within six months of joining the dole queue are highest when they use informal job search channels rather than the local employment office.'

One suggestion made by Perri6 and Lawson is that TECs purchase places on training courses which businesses are already running for their own employees. This would allow unemployed people to extend their social networks. They also recommend that employers who have signed up to the New Deal take steps to ensure that the unemployed people they appoint come into contact with as many other employees as possible:

'Welfare-to-work schemes need to be designed to ensure that participants make as many new contacts as possible during the six months of subsidised work or environmental volunteering the government has promised. If they do not emerge with any new connections their employment prospects will be little improved and their social exclusion will not have been reduced. The aim should be to make welfare-to-work an institution for social mixing.'

Relaxing benefit rules

Despite evidence that they usually engage in learning programmes which they hope will improve their job prospects, many unemployed people have been prevented from enrolling on courses or obliged to abandon those they have started, because they have been deemed unavailable for work (Rolfe *et al*, 1996). Anxiety about loss of benefit is a powerful deterrent to participation. Lindley (1991) has argued convincingly that the fear of putting a relatively stable financial situation at risk, the difficulty of finding jobs and the insecurity of the jobs available, combine to 'immobilise' many unemployed individuals. There is a strong case, therefore, for making it easier for people on benefit to study by relaxing the current rules which allow those on Job Seekers' Allowance to study for a specified number of guided hours a week (currently 16), on condition that they are available to take full-time work. The rule has been inconsistently applied by different Benefit Offices and there are welcome proposals in the Green Paper, *The Learning Age*, to review them and allow long-term unemployed individuals to undertake full-time courses without jeopardising their welfare benefits. Workskill pilots involving alternative, more flexible approaches that enable unemployed people to study and take part-time work have already been introduced in Leeds and Liverpool.

Dealing with Benefit Offices

Given that the threat to their precarious financial situation is one of the greatest barriers to the participation of unemployed men, education providers need to help and advise this group in their dealings with Benefit Offices. Some further education colleges have strict referral systems for handling enquiries from Benefit Offices about specific individuals. Only named persons and specific departments in the college are authorised to respond. One college liaises with the Employment Service and has invited Job Centre staff to view its job search facilities. The college has a *Jobshop* which is open five days a week and unemployed students who take advantage of the service are provided with individual files which are updated each time they attend. These are shown to Employment Service staff as evidence of job search (Donnelly, 1997).

Voluntary work

It would also help unemployed people if Benefit Offices treated volunteering as 'actively-seeking work'.

There are welcome signs of recognition, at government level, that voluntary work can provide a valuable route into paid work by enabling individuals to acquire important personal and practical skills that significantly increase their employability. Elsdon's study (1995) found that involvement in local voluntary organisations had helped:

> 'an encouraging number of previously unqualified adults to enter the labour market...There is overwhelming evidence that the generic skills and attitudes which are most valued by respondents are also directly transferable to and valued in their occupations. Competence, confidence, interpersonal and organising skills and readiness to discharge responsibility make people better at almost any job. They also alter the persona they present to other people; they become more impressive as well as more effective. Respondents gave numerous examples of such skills and attitudes which had eased or indeed enhanced their performance at work, but the key word which was mentioned almost invariably was confidence: it was the confidence acquired through membership of the local voluntary organisation (LVO) which had enabled the skills and attitudes to develop, or to be deployed. Responsibility with the LVO invariably meant planning, organising, ability to discuss and to listen, to tolerate disagreement and to stand up for one's own point of view. More generic skills learned in organisations were systematic policy-making and long-term planning and organisation and study (...)

> Members of self-help groups learned skills such as systematic organisation which prepared them for the problems they were going to face (....) Perhaps the commonest experience under this heading was that of people who had learned organising, managerial and negotiating skills as officers and members of committees and who took them from the LVO to all forms of paid work and to elected office.' (Elsdon, 1995: 67)

Community regeneration schemes

In some areas there has been a strong attempt to involve local unemployed people in schemes that will help bring prosperity to the area.

Matson has the largest council housing estate in Gloucester. It is in an area with a very high unemployment rate and a disproportionate number of young single people and lone parent families. The **Matson Neighbourhood Project** started in 1990 and is funded from a variety of sources – local businesses, the city and county councils, the local Health Authority and the European Social Fund.

The project is committed to developing a strong community infrastructure and encouraging local people to help themselves through developing sustainable resources and networks. There are five main strands of activity – advice and representation; mental health; jobs, education and training; furniture recycling; and community support. The stress is on responsiveness to local people's needs. There is a shop-front advice centre where people are helped to find their own solutions to needs and problems, and home visits are available.

In the first year the advice centre was open, there were 778 enquiries about education and training, 3,500 vacancies were advertised, and over 100 people were helped with job search. In 1996-97, demand for advice services increased by 50 per cent and unemployment in Matson fell by 38 per cent, half of which is attributed to the project (NICEC, 1998).

Trafford shopping, catering and leisure centre opened in Manchester in 1998. Before its launch, an 'employment charter' was established to maximise training and career opportunities for local and unemployed people. The charter is the result of a partnership between Manchester TEC and South Trafford College, supported by Trafford Metropolitan Borough Council and the Employment Service. An integral part of the initiative has been the Trafford Centre Recruitment and Training Foundation which opened in 1997 to help local and unemployed people share 7,000 career opportunities. All applicants took the Trafford Centre Career Step – a 75-hour course which included an English Tourist Board 'Welcome Host' certificate recognised by the Open University and the Northern Council of Further Education. The course was free to those receiving Income Support or the Job Seekers' Allowance. Successful candidates were recommended for an interview with a Trafford Centre employer (TES, 3 October 1997).

Older men

Many of the unemployed are older men and surveys consistently show that participation in all forms of adult learning diminishes at age 50. This is true for both sexes but particularly for men, many of whom have already retired at this age. Ford (1997:5) refers to *'the rapidly accelerating emergence of 45 plus as a main career transition point for many members of the working population.'* Whether desired or not, retirement can be another stressful transition period for men since, like unemployment, it involves the loss of that which above all else provides male identity and status – paid work:

'For a large number, third-age career transition may prove at least as difficult as

young people's transition from education or training into work, but with the added difficulty of facing age demarcations and cut-off points. The adjustments required can be difficult and painful, with some — through skill, occupational background, personality and experience — being much better equipped to cope with the major life change than others (…) Where skills and experience no longer appear to fit the local labour market, there are additional hurdles to surmount, often requiring the identification of suitable learning opportunities for older students and trainees, or the development of new opportunities which can meet the needs of learners in the third age.' (Ford, 1997: 5)

Encouraging men who are no longer economically active to participate in learning programmes is a considerable challenge. Although educational activities could help them manage a difficult period of transition and find alternatives to full-time work, there are far more women aged over 50 engaged in learning than men of the same age.

Ford suggests that the first need of people who leave the labour market at 45 plus is for appropriate and high quality guidance which: *'could determine whether their future is one of continual individual growth and development or individual stagnation and decline'.* The role of such guidance would be to:

• explore with individuals ways in which they can continue to use their skills and experience and continue to make a contribution to society;
• provide information and advice on paid or voluntary employment, education, training and leisure activities;
• help people to reappraise their skills and strengths and devise an action plan for the future.

Some programmes are aimed specifically at older, redundant or prematurely retired individuals. Although targeted at both sexes, these can be of particular value to men who find it difficult to be without employment.

Third Age Challenge (TAC) which was launched in April 1995, promotes and supports projects that tackle age discrimination, creates opportunities for training and guidance and helps people over 45 to build their self-esteem and find secure employment. TAC has pioneered a New Directions course which involves work on life-mapping and networks; CVs and interview techniques; skills assessment; personal development; motivation; financial stocktaking and enterprise induction.

With the help of ESF funding, a version of the course has been produced an cassette and a Back on Track individual learning pack has also been produced to help individuals devise their own action plans. A training programme has also been developed to prepare trainers to deliver New Directions courses tailored to meet local needs.

TAC is also working with the DfEE on developing lifelong learning programmes for people aged 50-plus (Ford, 1997).

East Midlands Third Age Challenge which was established in 1996, offers free services to people aged 40 plus. These include career guidance, seminars and training programmes in areas such as CV preparation, interview techniques and job search. Links have also been established with local employers. During the first four months of operation, 103 people were helped back into employment, 49 into full-time further education and 56 advised on self-employment (Ford, 1997).

Future Prospects in York is a city-centre educational guidance service supported by York College of Further and Higher Education. The service has been providing individual support, guidance and mentoring to workers made redundant from a large railway engineering company. There are two support workers whose task is to befriend and help individuals who have lost confidence and self-esteem and to support them in identifying and applying for suitable education, training and work.

As well as holding open sessions in its city centre premises, Future Prospects arranges home visits and organises a social club which meets regularly at a local working men's club. The encouragement of peer-group support is considered very important (Ford, 1997).

The University of Central Lancashire has mounted a range of initiatives for older learners. These have included a range of vocational and informal learning programmes and the development of over 50 University of the Third Age groups across the North West. The University has also established a Preparation for Retirement programme, Gateways provision and guidance for older people and a series of summer events and activities targeted at them including IT, drama, art and languages (Ford, 1997).

The NIACE Older & Bolder initiative was launched in 1995 with funding from the Carnegie UK Trust and the Esmée Fairbairn Charitable Trust. The aim is to promote and develop the participation of adults aged 50-plus in mainstream and special learning programmes, both vocational and non-vocational. There is a specific focus on those who have lacked opportunities to continue learning. Older and Bolder is establishing a nationwide network to collate, disseminate and promote good practice in education with older adults. The project is especially concerned to promote initiatives which identify the learning needs of older adults within local communities, target those who do not have ready access to education and training, and achieve greater third age participation levels.

Non-work-related programmes

There appear to be few *non*-work-related education programmes targeted specifically at older men, although those who engage in learning often have a wider range of learning interests than younger men and are less motivated by the desire to enhance their employment prospects. Non-vocational programmes and activities for older learners are often targeted at both sexes which can lead to an imbalance since, as previously noted, women are likely to take advantage of them in greater numbers than men.

Voluntary activity

The activity levels and patterns of older men inevitably vary according to individual skills, circumstances and disposition. Some become involved in voluntary and community activities in order to continue making a contribution to society, and these activities can lead to involvement in learning and sometimes to employment. As with other 'joining' activities, there is evidence of a gender divide. One study (EC, 1997) has found that women volunteers tend to want to help those in need, by befriending and organising events, while men prefer to become involved in committees and administration.

The Retired and Senior Volunteer Programme (RSVP) is a version of Community Service Volunteers (CSV), with the emphasis on encouraging older people to become volunteers in their communities. There are over 150 organisers and coordinators across the country and nearly 4,000 volunteers who are engaged in a variety of projects including activities in arts and crafts, supporting older people, conservation and the environment, helping young people, health and welfare.

The role of the regional coordinators is to encourage volunteering, recruit volunteers, identify and support projects and groups and to provide guidance. In the Yorkshire region, the coordinator has worked with the National Union of Miners to encourage and help older redundant miners to volunteer and create projects in their communities (Ford, 1997).

Minority ethnic group men

The findings of a survey of minority ethnic participation (Sargant, 1993) suggested that learning programmes for men in different ethnic communities need to be practical and vocational in response to their preference for useful and employment-related skills.

Given the diversity of ethnic groups, specific targeted approaches will be required to recruit different groups of men, involving outreach workers and tutors from the same community. Research into community characteristics and needs may also be required to identify the most appropriate and effective educational approaches with men from the different communities.

Coventry Bangladeshi Centre, located in the inner city, provides a variety of social and employment and training-related services to the Bangladeshi community. The centre has been successfully running women's training programmes but has experienced difficulty recruiting men to programmes designed for them. Discussion with colleagues in PACT (Partnership, Action and Change through Training) led to the decision to train a small group of men from the Asian community to conduct research into male learning needs and identify how the centre could make an adequate response. A project was subsequently set up which aimed to extend participants' communication skills and train them in community-based research skills. They could gain Open College Network accreditation and progress to education, training or paid employment in community action and development. Participants had the opportunity to contribute to the design of their own programme as well as to identify what further training and community projects could be developed.

Participants in the programme worked on their listening and communication skills and conducted action research into their own community. They discovered that most unemployed Bangladeshi men were unwilling to commit themselves to a regular weekly training session even when they were interested in the subject. As a result of the research findings, some drop-in training has been organised at the centre in areas such as IT. However, drop-in learning is not appropriate for all subjects and the centre is now considering providing a mixture of community and employment development activities, as well as guidance provision, alongside the drop-in training. Some group work programmes are also planned, to complement the drop-in sessions.

The project integrated action research and core skills. This enhanced the skills of learners as well as benefiting the community as a whole. Some participants went on to study in further and higher education and three went on to help Coventry University in a further piece of research within the Bangladeshi community (PACT, 1997).

Partnerships

Some ethnic groups have been so badly served by the education system that a multi-pronged partnership approach is needed to encourage their greater participation.

Birmingham TEC works with nine different community groups and has a particular focus on the African-Caribbean community with whom it has established a partnership. There are four sub-groups covering education, employment, training and enterprise. The groups have agreed priorities for an action plan. These include:
• developing the capacity of members of the African-Caribbean community to serve as parent governors in schools;
• setting up a mentoring programme targeting young African-Caribbeans at risk of exclusion from education or under-achieving in school;

- encouraging African-Caribbean employers to train and develop their staff, especially young people;
- setting up a bursary scheme, part-funded by the TEC, to subsidise African-Caribbeans wishing to undertake education or training (NACETT, 1997a).

Mentor schemes

Mentor schemes can be an effective means of increasing participation among members of ethnic communities.

Two colleges, **North London** and **City College Manchester**, have established mentor projects to increase participation among African-Caribbean men and improve their access to academic and employment opportunities.

The Manchester scheme which is supported by European funding, collaborates with a number of partners including Manchester Metropolitan University, an enterprise agency which provides support for young male ex-offenders and the probation service. As part of the project, black male students were invited to become involved in the mentoring service and this has led to a reduction in non-completion rates.

In 1997, a summer workshop roadshow was held to raise awareness of the programmes and mentoring support available for African-Caribbean men at the college. The roadshow took place over three days at three different locations in the Manchester area. It involved three workshops. The first, on music technology and jungle music, provided hands-on experience and information on courses, qualifications and jobs in the music industry. The second focused on IT with a demonstration of the Internet system, hands-on experience and information on courses, qualifications and jobs within the IT industry. The third provided information on mentor support, career advice, black Access and Making your Experience Count. There was also a speaker on educational opportunities.

The roadshow was publicised through local radio, the BBC and Granada TV, posters and leaflets. It attracted between 50 and 60 men aged from their early teens to 45 years old. All received an information pack on the three workshops and information on the courses available in the three major colleges in Manchester. Twenty-five of them identified courses they were interested in and there were 10 immediate enrolments and 15 potential ones. The main interests expressed were in the performing arts (music) and Black Access (Sheriffe, 1997).

Self-help

Frontline Community Self-Build was set up seven years ago by three unemployed black men, to help others in the Chapeltown and Harehills community to develop skills and self-reliance. They set themselves three goals. The first was to make a success of building their own homes; the second was to set up a construction company; and the third was to develop a training arm for the company.

The group successfully completed the NEBSM (National Examining Board in Supervisory Management) Introductory course which gave them the know-how and self-confidence to set up their own company. The course was run at Thomas Danby College in conjunction with Chapeltown Business Services and customised to meet the needs of people wishing to become self-employed. The group have since tackled the full NEBSM Certificate programme. They see themselves as positive role models for other unemployed black adults, and have encouraged a number of other Frontline members to undertake training programmes including NVQs in construction and supervisor/management. (Source: NIACE, 1996, Adult Learners' Week Awards)

Ex-offenders

An in-house charity, **The Blantyre House Vocational Fund**, offers men who reside in Blantyre House Prison the opportunity for vocational training in preparation for work once their sentences have ended. The Fund is targeted at prisoners serving sentences of five years or more (including those nearing the end of life sentences). The range of learning opportunities offered include construction teaching, road transport, car maintenance, art and design, and are complemented by the delivery of key skills and education and career guidance.

Individual learning needs are identified through initial discussions with inmates and tutors, probation representatives and security staff subsequently work together to support the learners' goals. A programme is formally agreed and a contract signed by the prisoner and an education/training representative. Additional funding for the programme is sought from charities with a contribution from the prisoner.

The main benefits of the programme have been identified as changed attitudes and cessation of offending. Some recipients of the programme have progressed to working for charitable organisations, while others have gone back into education. (Source: NIACE, 1998, Adult Learners' Week New Opportunities Awards)

A mentoring scheme which is run by **Dorset Probationary Service** aims to equip ex-offenders who have been on probation orders or community service sentences with skills to help them get a job. All are handicapped by having a criminal record, and many also lack basic literacy and number skills. Clients are matched with a mentor who works with them, usually in one-to-one sessions, through an agreed action plan.

Many of the jobs now available in the area are in the hotel industry, and the main courses pursued are the ASDAN foundation training and Further Education core skills awards in areas such as basic food hygiene, first aid, and health and safety certificates. During 1995, 150 clients completed the programme and one aged 42 won Dorset TEC's 1995 Trainee of the

Year award, competing against every other further education student in the county. (Source: NIACE, 1996, Adult Learners' Week Awards)

• • •

The examples outlined above illustrate how sensitive, targeted approaches can result in increased involvement in learning by the male groups who are least represented in formal education and training.

Table 36. Main source of information about current/recent learning, United Kingdom, 1996

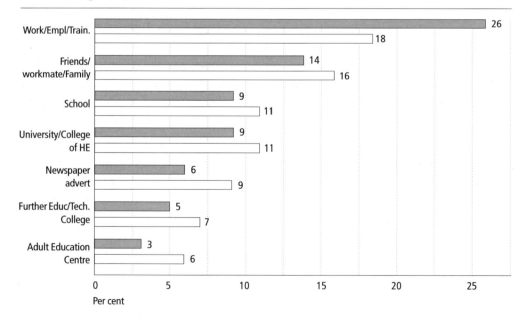

Per cent

Source: NIACE/Gallup survey commissioned by DfEE

Note: Figures for sample aged over 17 in the UK in 1996.

CHAPTER SIX

Conclusions

Men as a whole are not 'missing' from post-school education and training: statistics show that when all forms of learning are taken into account they participate in slightly greater numbers than women. However, men tend to have different learning priorities and interests than women and they frequent fewer education sectors. Some male groups are significantly under-represented in all forms of post-compulsory education and training, notably those with fewest qualifications and skills, early school leavers with a history of exclusion or poor school attendance, manual workers, older men, some black minority ethnic groups.

Work-related motives

Studies consistently indicate that work is a key motivator for men and that those who engage in education and training do so largely for practical, and employment-related reasons.

That male participation is driven largely by motivations to do with employment is not surprising since it is work which, more than anything else, provides men with identity and status. The predominantly instrumental focus of educational policy in recent years has inevitably reinforced the pattern and it may take some time for it to change to any significant degree. As Alan Tuckett (1997: 32) argued in relation to the anticipated policy paper on lifelong learning (which emerged as the Green Paper, *The Learning Age*): *'It will need more than a single policy document to shift the instrumentalism of the past few years.'* Despite the welcome recognition in The Learning Age of the value, wider purposes and benefits of learning, this emphasis largely remains. Promoting 'employability' is a key theme in domestic and European policy to raise skill levels and reduce 'social exclusion'.

Employability

Ostensibly, this emphasis is highly relevant to the male groups who tend not to participate in education and training since one of their main characteristics is to be outside or on the margins of the labour market. They are young men without qualifications who have never had a job; low-skilled manual workers who are intermittently and casually employed; minority ethnic men who have difficulty obtaining jobs; men over 40 who have been made redundant or obliged to take premature retirement.

Employability is a useful concept and it is vitally important to help those who are unqualified, low skilled and otherwise disadvantaged in the labour market to gain the necessary skills and competencies to obtain jobs. But it has the connotation that people are to blame for their own predicament. Unemployment and insecure employment are not always the result of individuals' lack of requisite skills, qualifications and flexibility, but of a whole range of factors – business down-sizing and restructuring, changes in markets, lack of investment, ageism in the labour market, long-term sickness and disability, to name but a few. Racism is another factor. Men from the black minority ethnic groups experience acute difficulties in finding employment and there is evidence of a shameful discrimination against them in the labour force. (The setting up of a new advisory body – the Race, Employment and Education Forum [REEF] – to advise on how to improve opportunities for black and Asian individuals is a welcome response to this situation.)

The stress on individual employability also fails to take account of the lack of job opportunities in some areas. Increased participation in education and training by the people most affected by unemployment will not make up for the effects of political neglect and the lack of investment in some cities and regions. As Webster (1997a) argues, long-term unemployment cannot be blamed on the victims but on the loss of jobs, a shortage of which persists in precisely those areas where the largest number have disappeared. There is now a widespread view that job creation is needed in both the private and public sectors to alleviate high levels of male unemployment. The report *Employment in Europe 1996* (EC, 1996) warns that a high level of educational attainment is not a guarantee of employment and that the rise in the number of people with qualifications without a commensurate rise in the number of skilled jobs available makes life even harder for those with few or low-level qualifications. Webster (1997a) argues that the real solution to joblessness is the creation of 'blue collar jobs': *'Getting people off welfare and into work is certainly a valid objective. But the way to achieve it is not through "welfare to work" measures as currently conceived. These offer an illusory "short cut" in which long-term unemployment can supposedly be cut without actually addressing joblessness. Long-term unemployment will fall in each area in line with total unemployment as and when more suitable jobs become available in that area.'*

Any suggestion that participation in education and training is the principal solution to unemployment therefore lacks credibility and risks raising false hopes, especially among the long-term unemployed. This does not mean that training programmes for the unemployed should not be developed or expanded, but that they should be based on a realistic understanding of the labour market and lead to proper jobs.

The New Deal for unemployed people is considerably more wide-ranging and comprehensive than its predecessors and the Gateway period has an important role in helping unemployed people to choose appropriate routes into education, training and voluntary or paid employment. However, the programme will only benefit people if, to quote Coffield (1997: 85): *'it encourages Lifelong Learning and does not lead to dead-end jobs without training or prospects, as in the past'.* Unemployed men may be reluctant to join yet another scheme unless it can be seen to genuinely increase job prospects, and any elements of compulsion can be counter-productive.

Moreover there are still anxieties among those receiving the Job Seeker's Allowance about jeopardising their benefits if they engage in part-time learning. For a number of years, this fear has acted as a significant brake on unemployed men's readiness to engage in education programmes. Their levels of participation would increase if it were made easier for them to enrol in programmes without threat to their benefits, and if benefit officers recognised learning as an appropriate pre-employment activity. This would be logical since there is evidence that unemployed people usually enrol in programmes which they believe will improve their chances in the labour market. Despite attempts by the Government to clarify the relationship between the New Deal and the 16-hour rule, there are fears that since the former is pitched at people with qualifications below level 2, unemployed individuals may be discouraged from taking higher level study such as Access to higher education courses. On this point DfEE guidance states that there might be a: *'small minority of cases where the personal advisor considers that existing study does not enhance the jobseeker's employability and (…) the client will be unable to continue the course during their New Deal training time.'*

Attracting the missing groups

Many of the men who engage least in learning are unemployed or under-employed and are experiencing problems which appropriate learning opportunities might help them to manage. However, they are prevented from engaging in education by a combination of powerful deterrents: structural constraints and institutional rigidities; scepticism about the value of learning and strongly held views about what constitutes appropriate male behaviour.

Men's attitudes to education are bound up with the traditional role they have been socialised into expecting and wanting, and into which many are still locked by male cultural norms and values. Their readiness to participate in learning is often inhibited by a reluctance to expose lack of knowledge and express needs and fixed views on male and female roles in society. Learning is perceived by some groups as a process that ends on leaving school and as a feminine rather than masculine activity. Studies have revealed a strongly held conviction among men in some working-class communities that it is appropriate for women to take part in education but not for themselves. As one tutor was told: *'it's alright for our lass but not for us'.* As the number of women participating in education and training increases, this view tends to be reinforced.

Some men cling to outmoded gender stereotypes despite the considerable changes that have taken place in society and in the nature and structures of employment. Although the economic and social transformations of recent years have brought about some adjustments in thinking and attitudes, the most difficult change to make is in their relationship with, and (over) attachment to, work. This presents a considerable challenge to the creation of a lifelong learning culture. As long as the idea of returning to education or training at a mature age is viewed by (some) men as humiliating and a step back rather than forwards, it will be difficult to persuade them to participate. To change such attitudes requires a cultural transformation of which there is as yet little sign.

Changing male culture

A starting point would be for learning to be promoted and seen as a normal and acceptable male activity from an early age. The evidence is that, as a society, we have signally failed to convey to boys, especially those from a working-class background, the value and relevance of education and the critical link between educational attainment and future prospects. This is demonstrated in the preliminary findings of a research project showing that twice as many boys as girls plan to leave school and seek employment at age 16 (Tyesome, 1998).

The problem of low aspiration and under-achievement among boys has been attributed to a number of factors: family background and economic circumstances; current school practices and assessment systems, and the under-valuing of vocational learning . But it is also the result of socially constructed ideas of masculinity and perceptions of the interdependence of masculinity and work. The preoccupation with paid work now needs to be questioned, for: *'not only are the employment and financial returns increasingly hard to predict, but it can limit, or damage, other parts of life of equal, or ultimately greater importance.'* (Moss, 1996: 246)

We cannot expect education by itself to change a situation created and sustained by the wider culture. Nevertheless it does have a potential role in helping boys and men to adjust their expectations, not only of the role employment will play in their lives, but also of the kind of work they will do: *'People have got to offer what is wanted. These days it's not being able to hammer a nail in but being able to talk to people.'* (Worker at a training centre in Newcastle upon Tyne, cited in Tyler, 1997)

Education can encourage men to seek a better balance between work, family and leisure, and find dignity, satisfaction and status through means other than paid employment, and particularly through parenthood. Moss (1996: 247) describes the growing *'feminisation of childhood'* as a worrying feature of modern life and argues that we need to encourage and promote more participation by men in the care and upbringing of children: '*on the basis that greater male investment in child-rearing, and a better balance in men's lives between employment and family responsibilities, will be good — not only for men, but for children, their partners and the wider society*'. However, the same cultural and structural forces that lock men into employment as their main *raison d'être*, prohibit their greater involvement in childcare: the persisting belief that childcare is the exclusive responsibility of women reinforced by factors such as job insecurity, long working hours, lack of paternity leave and absence of relevant role models: '*The media currently tends to depict them [fathers] either as the angst-ridden dads of Thirty Something or as incompetent "dorks" populating television advertisements for washing liquids or fish fingers.*' (Baker, 1996: 37)

Targeted provision

Appropriate targeted programmes can help men to manage different life stages and periods of transition. However, the evidence suggests that insufficient efforts are being made to encourage non-participating men to engage in learning. Although there is a range of initiatives targeted at young unemployed people and different groups (such as young offenders) who are predominately male, there are relatively few programmes aimed specifically at men over 25, especially those with no qualifications and low skills. There is widespread recognition that women need help to reassess their situation and future options, and providers now routinely offer some programmes for those who are at a stage when they wish to return to education or work or just make a change in their lives. There is a strong case for providing similar programmes for men, especially those experiencing change and disruption in their lives, to help them identify their strengths, reassess their priorities and future direction, and develop new interests and skills. This is *not* to suggest that resources should be directed away from programmes for women — any measures taken to increase men's participation should not be at the expense of women's opportunities — but that alongside programmes for women there should be some that are targeted at men. Some providers are already organising men-only courses and, although there can be initial recruitment problems, the signs are that men appreciate learning in an all-male environment.

However, the recruitment of under-represented men to targeted learning activities will depend on perceptions of their value and relevance . Men need to know that participating in learning will have practical 'pay-offs' and will neither stigmatise them nor be detrimental to their interests.

Studies also suggest that programmes targeted at men need to have clearly focused content and objectives and involve 'doing' rather than talking. Some of the most effective initiatives for young men, for example, have involved activities such as sports, building cars and learning to drive.

Information technology – a popular curriculum area with adults of both sexes – has a potentially huge role in attracting men to learning. Boys and men like using computers: their performance is not 'on show' to others and they receive instant results and feedback.

Presentation and delivery

It is well established that many people prefer to make their return to learning in a familiar, local venue. Many men who would never have considered approaching an education centre or college have been attracted back to non-institutionalised learning through initiatives in workplaces, pubs, clubs and sports centres. To achieve wider male participation, adult and further education institutions need to appoint more male outreach development workers and more male 'frontline' (reception, guidance) staff as well as tutors. This will help to counteract their increasingly feminised image.

The programmes that have been most effective in attracting non-participant men have usually been presented and delivered in particular ways. The former REPLAN project's programmes for the adult unemployed, collaborative employee development schemes, innovative college outreach programmes and a wide range of special projects have demonstrated that men from groups that habitually do not engage in learning can be motivated to participate in a wide range of education programmes when these are presented in ways that do not threaten their status and dignity; targeted at peer groups rather than individuals; delivered in places that men frequent during their work or leisure time; flexible and not constrained by rigid institutional arrangements or funding regimes and when they promise outcomes which appear to justify expenditure of money, time and effort and outweigh any psychological costs such as fear of failure. As with programmes for women, the most effective programmes for men do not use an approach that suggests skill and knowledge deficiencies but promise from the start to recognise and build on existing knowledge and skills This protects individual self-esteem.

Adequate resourcing

Many of the most effective approaches have been outside mainstream practice and funded on a short-term basis. This can be counter-productive. Short-term funding and competitive bidding restrict the amount that can be achieved and create enormous pressures for organisers and tutors. Those working with non-traditional learners find that it can take a considerable period to achieve results because of the time it takes to develop confidence and trust. According to one tutor: *'There are no quick fixes. Consistency and long-term involvement are a must in these communities.'* Although short-term projects can help some non-traditional learners to access education and training, they cannot succeed in changing overall participation patterns.

Partnership

Many of the most effective education initiatives for men are examples of inter-agency collaboration. Partnership is now considered of utmost importance in widening participation and combating social exclusion, and the concept could usefully be extended to the ways in which government departments themselves liaise and collaborate with each other. To widen participation on a large scale requires greater coordination between education and employment policies; and health, social services and transport policies. Although this is happening to some extent with Welfare to Work and the Prime Minister has promised us 'joined-up government', there is still a danger of some departmental policies conflicting with one another. It has been pointed out, for example, that there may be some contradiction between the New Deal and the National Minimum Wage (Bewick, 1997b: 24)

Help with costs

Financial considerations affect participation at all ages. Since high adult unemployment puts pressure on young people, especially boys, to leave school early and start earning, it should be made more financially attractive for young people from low income families to continue in education after the age of 16. According to research findings from Northern Ireland, this would help to break the inter-generational cycles of low skills and poor educational attainment (Armstrong, 1997). The proposed pilot maintenance grants for those aged 16-18 are a welcome step in this direction.

The costs of learning also deter adults (as is demonstrated in the drop in numbers of mature students applying for higher education since the loss of grants and imposition of tuition fees). The Report of the Further Education Student Support Advisory Group on arrangements for effective student support in further education (DfEE, 1998d) identified as its main concerns the extent to which the availability of financial support varies in different parts of the country; the 'dramatic' fall in expenditure on discretionary awards for further education; the virtual absence of financial support for adult students, and the lack of clarity and consistency about people's entitlement to state benefits when they are in education.

There are a number of ways in which student funding systems might be changed to assist the participation of non-traditional learners. NIACE has frequently argued that, to widen participation and create a lifelong learning culture, there is a need to treat and fund part-time students on the same basis as full-time ones. Extra funding allocations for students from specific postcodes, as provided by the Further Education Funding Councils and proposed by the Higher Education Funding Council for England, is a way of encouraging institutions to recruit students from more disadvantaged backgrounds. The extension of tax relief to people involved in a wider spectrum of learning activities would be another means of widening participation. Two new government initiatives – an increase in the access funds available in the FE sector and individual learning accounts (ILAs) – may also attract new learners. However, at the time of writing, there are a number of unanswered questions about ILAs: how will individuals on low incomes be persuaded to dedicate money from already scant resources for this purpose, especially if they perceive little value or relevance in education? How will employers who do not currently invest in their workers be persuaded to contribute to the accounts? Will all adults be eligible for the accounts, irrespective of age? How can the accounts widen participation without a substantial increase in investment in guidance services?

Why should we attempt to widen participation?

At this point it is pertinent to reconsider the question raised earlier: why should we try and increase demand for education and training among men who have no apparent interest in participating? It is frequently pointed out that people engage in informal learning throughout their lives and those who lack formal qualifications often have knowledge and skills in abundance. For many of those outside the workforce, the priority is not education but finding a job. For those in employment who have experienced an increase in workload and working hours: *the prospect of lifelong learning may be interpreted as more of a burden, as more akin to a lifelong sentence than an invitation to personal growth and development.'* (Coffield, 1997: 87)

Thus, it might be argued that we should respect people's choices and make no efforts to attract those who habitually do not engage in formal learning into education or training programmes. This argument would only be sustainable if there were not such clear social class divisions in current participant profiles, which are attributable not just to individual lack of interest and motivation but to a range of interacting cultural, material and structural obstacles.

Unequal learning opportunities

The current structures and funding of post-school education and training can result, albeit unintentionally, in blocking access to less advantaged segments of the adult population, as can the image and environment of some education institutions. Some post-school education and training providers have not sufficiently broadened their appeal to under-represented groups. If adult education centres continue to be staffed and attended mainly by women, then men will not frequent them in large numbers. If colleges are still largely oriented towards young people in their ethos and practices, then less confident learners over the age of 25 will feel intimidated by them. If universities are believed to cater exclusively for more affluent and 'clever' social groups, then low income groups will not consider applying. (In this respect, some worry that the developing University for Industry, which has a potentially valuable role in helping non-learners to access different forms of education and training, has retained a title that may be off-putting to individuals from a manual work background.)

In many countries, adult education opportunities are increasingly linked to work. Secondary analysis of data produced by the International Adult Literacy Study has revealed that employer-supported activities are making a growing contribution to overall adult education opportunities, particularly in the UK and the US. The data showed that in the UK, two out of three adult learners participate in courses supported by a employer (Rubenson, 1998). Because of the unevenness in employer practice, there are wide inequalities in provision:

'As adult education becomes increasingly linked to work, strategies for lifelong learning for all must recognise the inequality in receiving employer support for education and training.' Persons outside the labour market or in undemanding jobs are clearly up against a barrier with regard to both learning itself and their readiness for it. (...) The analyses show that the likelihood of an employee receiving some support for education and training from the employer is related to the size of the company one happens to be working in, occupational status and the engagement in literacy activities at work. In general, it is a handicap to work in a small or medium-sized company when it comes to benefiting from employer-supported education and training.' (Rubenson, 1998: 262)

In Britain, men's participation in learning would be significantly increased if there were a more effective national framework for learning in the workplace. Although the most common source of funded learning opportunities for men is their employer, it is estimated that about 40 per cent of workers, usually older ones and those with the lowest skill levels, receive no employer-supported training. Given this finding and the perennial lamentations about low qualification levels, it is surprising that employers are still expected to train on a voluntary basis. It is also short-sighted: the economic reasons for training low skilled and older workers are compelling. According to population forecasts (DfEE, 1998b), by the year 2001, the overall number of people of working age over 35 will have increased by 9 per cent and the cohorts aged 35 to 44 and 55 to 59 will both have increased by 13 per cent. In contrast, the numbers of people aged between 16 and 19 will have increased by only 6 per cent and the numbers of those between 20 and 24 will have fallen by 5 per cent.

It is a cause for some regret, therefore, that stronger measures have not been introduced to encourage employers to train all their workers, particularly those over 35 and those who are low skilled. Some feel that too much onus for increasing employability is put on individuals and too little is required of corporate employers: *'The Government should transfer to employers the compulsion built into its new deal for young people. This could take the form of a compulsory levy or registration scheme with a membership fee so that corporations, which benefit from a skilled labour force do something towards creating one.'* (Bender 1997)

To reduce the scale of inequalities in provision, therefore, much needs to be done both in and outside employment. Previous research has made it abundantly clear that education has the ability to transform individual lives and that exposure to learning of any kind often leads to positive attitudes and the motivation to continue. It is essential in a civilised society, especially one which aspires to be a 'learning' society, that opportunities be made available to all who can be helped by them, not just to people who are already education-rich and can afford to pay. For men, these should not be narrowly focused on 'employability' and skills to help them adjust to the vagaries and changing requirements of an uncertain labour market. There should be a more balanced set of learning opportunities that will provide both the skills individuals need to gain employment and broader, self-development skills to help those outside the labour market lead fuller, more creative and satisfying lives.

Bibliography

Aggleton P, 1987, *Rebels without a cause?*, Lewes, Falmer Press

Armstrong D, 1997, *Staying on in full-time education in Northern Ireland: an economic analysis*, Department of Education Northern Ireland (DENI), Research Report Series 7

Atkin C, 1997, 'Who needs key skills anyway?', *'t' magazine*, June, 14-16

Audit Commission, 1996, *Misspent youth: young people and crime*, London, Audit Commission

Baker DP and Jones D, 1993, 'Creating gender equality: cross-national stratification and mathematical achievement', *Sociology of Education*, 66, 91-103

Baker P, 1996, 'Bringing the male crisis into the open' in Lloyd T and Wood T (eds) *What's next for men*, London, Working with Men, 28-40

Ball C, 1991, *Learning pays: the role of post-compulsory education and training*, Interim Report, April 1991, London, Royal Society of Arts/Industry Matters

Banks MH and Davies B, 1990, *Motivation, Unemployment and Employment Department programmes*, Research Paper 80, MRC/ESRC Social and Applied Psychology Unit, Department of Psychology, University of Sheffield

Barnard N, 1997a, 'To degrees the hard way', *Times Educational Supplement*, 19 September

Barnard N, 1997b, 'Young bear brunt of joblessness', *Times Educational Supplement*, 31 October

Barnard N, 1998a, 'Offenders to be taught the 3Rs', *Times Educational Supplement*, 22 February

Barnard N, 1998b, 'It wasn't like that in my day', *Times Educational Supplement*, 6 March

Bassett P, 1997, 'Women stay jobless for shorter time than men', *The Times*, 6 March

Baty P, 1998, 'AoC fears New Deal deters jobless from study', *Times Higher Educational Supplement*, 17 April

Beattie A, 1997, *Working people and lifelong learning: a study of the impact of an employee development scheme*, Leicester, NIACE

Bell I, Houston N and Heyes R, 1997, 'Workless households, unemployment and economic inactivity', *Labour Market Trends* 108/9, September, 339 -345

Bell J, 1998, 'Girls still lag behind boys in science', *Times Educational Supplement*, 6 March, 23

Bender S, 1997, 'Young, gifted and let down', *Times Educational Supplement*, 26 September

Bewick T, 1997-98, 'Mind the (jobs) gap', *Training Tomorrow*, 11/7, December/January, 13

Bewick, T, 1997a, 'Implementing the minimum wage and the New Deal' *Working Brief*, October, 24-26

Bewick T, 1997b, 'The learning conundrum', *Training Tomorrow*, 11/6, September, 14

Blackburn RM and Jarman J, 1993, 'Changing inequalities in access to British universities', *Oxford Review of Education*, 19, 2, 197-216

Blaxter M, 1990, *Health and lifestyle*, London, Tavistock/Routledge, 87-99

Blundell R, Dearden L, Goodman A and Reed H, 1997, *Higher education, employment and earnings in Britain*, London, Institute of Fiscal Studies

Burgess S and Propper C, 1998, 'Future wages of sin in a misspent youth', *Times Educational Supplement*, 3 April

Bynner J, Ferri E and Shepherd P, 1997, *Twenty something in the 1990s: getting on, getting by and getting nowhere*, London, Aldgate

Bynner J and Parsons S, 1997, *It doesn't get any better: the impact of poor basic skills on the lives of 37-year-olds*, London, the Basic Skills Agency

Callender C and Metcalf H, 1997, *Women and training: research report* RR35, Policy Studies Institute

Carlton E, 1998 'Cool junior is our dad and best friend', *Times Educational Supplement*, 27 February

Chadwick G, 1993, 'Towards a vision of recurrent education', *Journal of Access Studies*, 8, 1, Spring, 8-26

Chatrik B and Convery P, 1997, 'Trends in labour market participation of ethnic groups, 1984-1996', *Labour Market Trends*, August/September, 295-303

Chatrik B, 1997a, 'Campaigning for youth', *Training Tomorrow*, June, 26

Chatrik B, 1997b, 'Minorities losing out under Modern Apprenticeships', *Working Brief*, 87, August/September, 17-18

Chatrik B, 1997c, 'New Deal – fair deal?', *Youth Unemployment Bulletin*, Winter, 4-5

Chatrik B, 1997d, 'Will a New Deal for 16 and 17 year-olds be a fair deal?', *Working Brief*, 87, August/September, 14-15

Chaudhary V, 1998, 'Problems that arise when boys will be boys', *Education Guardian*, 6 January, 6

Clayton P, and Slowey M, 1997, *Was it worth it? Gender boundaries and the role of adult education in labour market progress and social participation.* Preliminary research report presented at the 27th annual SCUTREA conference, University of London, 1-3 July, 1997, Department of Adult and Continuing Education, University of Glasgow

Clennell S (ed), 1990, *Older students in Europe: a survey of older students in four European countries*, The Open University Regional Academic Services

Coffield F (ed), 1997, A national strategy for lifelong learning. Papers presented at the international conference research on lifelong learning: implications for policy and practice, held at the University of Newcastle 25-27 November 1996, Department of Education, University of Newcastle, 143

Commission for Racial Equality, 1997, *Employment and unemployment revised.* Factsheets, Commission for Racial Equality

Commission for Racial Equality, 1998, *We regret to inform you...*, Commission for Racial Equality

Community Education Development Centre (CEDC), 1997, *Network Update*, Spring, Community Education Development Centre

Connell RW, 1998, *Masculinities*, Cambridge, Polity Press

Connor H, La Valle I, Tackey N and Perrtman S, 1996, *Ethnic minority graduates: differences by degrees*, report 309, Falmer, Institute of Employment Studies

Convery P, 1997a, 'Labour market "slack" at five million', *Working Brief*, August-September, 27-28

Convery P, 1997b, 'The learning and earning report: a manifesto for the excluded', *Working Brief*, May, 17

Convery P, 1997c, 'A manifesto for the excluded', *Working Brief*, May, 17

Convery P, 1997d, 'Recovery in female employment not matched by males', *Working Brief*, June, 15

Convery P, 1998a, 'New Deal for the over-25s', *Working Brief*, June, 8

Convery P, 1998b, 'Strong employment growth is patchy', *Working Brief*, February, 23-24

Coward R, 1998, *Analysis: empowering Rita?* Transcript of a recorded documentary, 5/3/98, BBC 4 News and Current Affairs

Crace J, 1998, 'Footballers to the rescue', *Guardian Education*, 13 January

Crequer N, 1998, 'Helpline hits the button', *Times Educational Supplement*, 6 March

Crequer N, 1997, 'Second chance saloon', *Times Educational Supplement*, Business Links, 13 June

Crowther-Hunt E, 1997, 'New Deal must open doors for unskilled', *Times Educational Supplement*, 18 July

Dearden L, Machin S, Reed H and Wilkinson D, 1997, *Labour turnover and work-related training*, London, Institute of Fiscal Studies

Department for Employment, 1993, *Statistical Bulletin* 14/93, Department for Education

Department for Education and Employment (DfEE), 1996, *Labour Market Trends incorporating Employment Gazette*, Department for Education and Employment

DfEE, 1997a, *Government-supported training: England and Wales*, 447/97, 31 December, Department for Education and Employment

DfEE, 1997b, 'Government-supported training outcomes by trainee characteristics', *Statistical Services Bulletin*, 4/97, May, Department for Education and Employment

DfEE, 1997c, *Labour Market Trends incorporating Employment Gazette* Department for Education and Employment

DfEE, 1997d, *Results of the 1997 National Curriculum Assessments of 14 year olds in England: Key Stage 3*, Department for Education and Employment

DfEE, 1997e, *Separate tables: statistics on women and men in education, training and employment*, Department for Education and Employment

DfEE, 1998a, *Education and training statistics for the United Kingdom*, Department for Education and Employment

DfEE, 1998b, *Labour market and skills trends 1997-1998*, Department for Education and Employment

DfEE, 1998c, *Skills and Enterprise Executive*, 1, February, Department for Education and Employment

DfEE, 1998d, *Arrangements for Effective Student Support in Further Education.* Report of the Further Education Student Support Advisory Group, Department for Education and Employment

DENI, 1997, *Research Briefing*, RB5/97, December, Department of Education Northern Ireland

Dewson S, Irving P, Johnson C and Whitting G, 1997, 'Evaluation of the prevocational pilots: case studies', *Labour Market Trends*, October, 377-378

Dex S, and McCulloch A, 1997, 'Unemployment and training histories: findings from the family and working life survey', *Labour Market Trends*, 105, 11, November, 449-454

Donnelly C, 1997-98, 'Training for Work needs to focus on meeting education targets', *Working Brief*, December-January, 25-27

Donnelly C, 1997, 'Students and colleges frustrated by 21-hour rule', *Working Brief*, March, 10-14

Edwards A, 1997a, 'Fractions on t'shopfloor', *Times Educational Supplement*, 28 November

Edwards A, 1997b, 'Freed from life on benefit', *Times Educational Supplement*, 19 September

Edward A, 1997c, 'Hi-tech help for illiteracy at work', *Times Educational Supplement*, 28 November

Edwards A, 1997d, 'Where l stands for literacy', *Times Educational Supplement*, 22 August

Elsdon K with Reynolds J and Stewart S, 1995, *Voluntary organisations: citizenship, learning and change*, Leicester, NIACE

Epstein D, 1996, *Real boys don't work: underachievement, masculinity and the harassment of sissies.* Paper presented to the ESRC seminar series on gender and education: are boys now underachieving? Institute of Education, 15 November

Equal Opportunities Commission (EOC), 1994, *Black and ethnic minority women and men in Britain 1994*, Manchester, Equal Opportunities Commission

EOC, 1997, *Education and vocational training in England and Wales.* Briefings on women and men in Britain, Manchester, Equal Opportunities Commission

European Commission (EC), 1996, *Employment in Europe 1996*, Employment and Social Affairs, Luxembourg, Office for Official Publication of the European Communities, European Commission

EC, 1997, *Age becomes her: older women in the EU, Women of Europe*, dossier 45, May-July, European Commission

FE Now, 1997, *National targets to be lowered*, 39, September

Ford G, 1997, *Career guidance in the third age*, NICEC Project Report, Cambridge

Fryer R, 1997, *Learning for the twenty-first century: first report of the National Advisory Group for Continuing Education and Lifelong Learning*, London, National Advisory Group for Continuing Education and Lifelong Learning

Fuller A and Saunders M, 1990, *The potential take up of mass training*, University of Lancaster, Association for Education and Training Technology's International Conference, University of Lancaster

Further Education Unit, 1985, *Consett: a case study of education and unemployment*

Gallagher AM, 1997, *Educational achievement and gender: a review of research evidence on the apparent underachievement of boys*, Research Report Series 6, DENI (Department of Education Northern Ireland), Bangor, Northern Ireland

Gardener S, 1997, 'Dreaming of a White Paper', *Adults Learning* September, 14

Ghouri N, 1998, 'Boys focus of literacy hotline', *Times Educational Supplement*, 20 February

Gipps C and Murphy P, 1997, *Equity in the classroom: towards effective pedagogy for girls and boys*, Falmer Press/UNESCO

Glennerster H, 1998, 'Does poor training make people poor?', *Times Educational Supplement*, 27 February

Government Statistical Service, 1990, *Criminal statistics England and Wales*, HMSO

Government Statistical Service, 1998, 'Qualifications data in the Labour Force Survey', *Labour Market Trends*, 106/1, January

Grainger RW, 1979, 'Working class mature students in full-time education', *Adult Education*, 52, 237-242

Grant L, 1998, 'Girls on top form', *The Guardian*, 6 January

Hackett G, 1998, 'Browsing around for the right courses', *Times Educational Supplement*, 6 March

Hampshire M, 1997, 'Mills of the mind', *Times Educational Supplement* 23 May

Hand A, Gambles J and Cooper E, 1994, *Individual commitment to learning: individuals' decision-making about lifetime learning*, Employment Department

HEFCE, *Widening access to higher education: a report by the HEFCE advisory groups of access and participation*, Higher Education Funding Council for England, 1996

HMI, 1992, *The preparation of girls for adult and working life*, HMSO, Her Majesty's Inspectorate

HMSO, 1996, *Social Trends 26: 1996 Edition*,

Hoare S, 1997, 'Link to the future', *Guardian Education*, 9 December

Hutton W, 1996, *The State we're in*, London, Vintage

IES, 1997, *Employment, unemployment and labour market disadvantage: summary of current research*, Institute for Employment Studies

Ireson J, 1998, 'Setting standards', *Times Educational Supplement*, 9 January

Julius C, 1998, 'Trainers score in extra time', *Times Educational Supplement*, 13 March

Karn V (ed), 1996, *Ethnicity in the 1991 census volume 4: employment, education and housing among the ethnic minority populations of Britain*, Office for National Statistics

Kennedy H, QC, 1997, *Learning works: widening participation in further education*, Coventry, Further Education Funding Council

Kimmel M, 1996, in Lloyd T and Wood T (eds), 'What's next for men?', London, *Working with Men*, 41-54

Lane M, 1998, 'How to turn the new lads into new men', *Guardian Education*, 13 January

Lindley RM, 1991, 'Individuals, human resources and markets' in Stevens J and Mackay R (eds), *Training and competitiveness*, NEDO Policy Issues Series, Kogan Page

Lloyd T, 1996, *Young men's health: a youth work concern*, London, Working with Men

Lloyd T and Wood T (eds), 1996, *What's next for men?* London, Working with Men

Lunneborg P, 1997, *OU men: work through lifelong learning*, Lutterworth Press

Mac an Ghaill M, 1996, 'What about the boys? Schooling, class and crisis masculinity', *Sociological Review*, 380-397

Macintosh M, 1990, 'Second time pupils: the return of women to school' in Fewell J and Paterson F, *Girls in their prime: Scottish education revisited*, Edinburgh, Scottish Academic Press

Mackay R (eds), *Training and competitiveness*, NEDO Policy Issues Series, Kogan, 210-220

Maclagen I, 1997a, 'Cut in YT hours may open door for unscrupulous training providers', *Working Brief*, July, 5

Maclagen I, 1997b, 'Combating exclusion – an innovative project', *Youth Unemployment Bulletin*, Winter, 9-10

Maclagan I, 1997c, 'Zero job, zero training, zero status', *Working Brief*, March

Maguire M, 1997, 'Employee development schemes: panacea or passing Fancy?' in Coffield F (ed), *op cit*, 143-157

Marshall B, 1997, 'Glasgow: real work with real training and support', *Working Brief*, April, 15-16

McGivney V, 1992a, *Motivating unemployed adults to undertake education and training*, Leicester, NIACE

McGivney V (ed), 1992b, *Opening colleges to adult learners*, Leicester, NIACE

McGivney V, 1997, *Evaluation of Gloucester primary health care project*, GLOSCAT (unpublished)

McIntyre J, 1998, *Perspectives from Australia.* Paper presented at the international symposium, rethinking participation research in adult education at the 39th annual adult education research conference, San Antonio, May 15-16

Merton, 1997a, *A lifeline for the lost generation*, NIACE, unpublished

Merton 1997b, 'Still disaffected after all these years', *Adults Learning*, February, 153-155

Mid Glamorgan TEC, 1996, *16 and 17 year olds in Mid Glamorgan not in education, training or employment*, Pontypridd, Mid Glamorgan

Midgeley S, 1997a, 'A chance to be Mr Motivated', *Times Educational Supplement*, 17 October

Midgeley S, 1997b, 'A framework for the future', *FE Now*, September

Midgeley S, 1997c, 'Putting the IT in community', *FE Now*, June

Midwinter E, (undated) *Thriving people, the growth and prospects of the U3A in the UK: an independent evaluation for the Calouste Gulbenkian Foundation*, UK Branch

Millar C, 1998, 'Hope and charity', *The Guardian*, 14 March, 7

Millard L, 1998, 'The male wail: life's no joke for a bloke', *Evening News*, 17 April

Morgan M, 'Working with disaffected youth', *Basic Skills*, September/October, 17-19

Moss P, 1996, 'Increasing men's involvement with their children' in Lloyd T and Wood T (eds) 1996, *op cit*, 243-251

Murphy P and Elwood J, 1996, *Gendered experiences, choices and achievement: exploring the limits*. Paper presented to the ESRC seminar series: gender and education: are boys now underachieving?, Institute of Education, London

Murphy P, 1998, 'Boys are not the only ones to lose out', *Guardian Education*, 13 January

Murray I, 1997, 'Jobsearch changes depriving unemployed of programme places', *Working Brief*, July

Murray I, 1998a, 'Barriers to self-employment for the unemployed', *Working Brief*, February

Murray I, 1998b, 'Labour sets out its policy to help adult long-term unemployed', *Working Brief*, December-January

NACETT, 1997a, *Developing a local targets strategy: a practical guide*, National Advisory Council for Education and Training Targets

NACETT, 1997b, *Skills for 2000: report on progress towards the National Targets For Education and Training*, National Advisory Council for Education and Training Targets, August

Nash, I, 1997a, 'Colleges to take over sixth forms', *Times Educational Supplement*, 29 August

Nash I, 1997b, 'Volunteers succeed in escaping the dole queue', *Times Educational Supplement*, 13 June

Nash I, 1997c, 'Why jobseekers shun the fast buck', *Times Educational Supplement*, FE Focus, 19 September

Nash, I, 1998, 'Early retirement "drains" Britain', *Times Educational Supplement*, 17 April

National Committee of Enquiry into Higher Education, 1997, *Higher education in the learning society: report of the National Committee*, London, National Committee of Enquiry into Higher Education

NICEC, 1998, *Adult guidance in community settings*, NICEC briefing, Cambridge, National Institute for Careers Education and Counselling

NOCN, 1996, *Annual report 1995/96*, Derby, University of Derby, National Open College Network

Neville C, 1994, 'Achille's heel', *Adults Learning*, April, 207-209

Neville C, 1996, Men in education: a study of participant and non -participant men in continuing education, MPhil dissertation, University of Bradford

New Deal Secretariat, 1997, *New Deal for young unemployed people: background briefing notes*

NIACE/NYA, 1998, Young Adult Learners' Project, *Clued In*, 2, March, Leicester, NIACE

Noble D, 1994, 'Let them eat skills', *The Review of Education Pedagogy, Cultural Studies*, 16, 1, 15-29

North Yorkshire TEC, 1997, *The participation of men in education and training: what have you got to lose?* A Further Education Development Fund Project executive report, May, Harrogate College, North Yorkshire Training and Enterprise Council

O'Shea J and Corrigan P, 1979, 'Surviving adult education', *Adult Education*, 52, 4

O'Sullivan J, 1998, 'Playing the game: champions of field and class', *The Independent*, 15 January

Ochert A, 1998, 'Why poor means poorly and wealth buys health', *The Times Higher*, 27 March

Partnership, Action and Change through Training (PACT), 1997, *Case Studies*, Partnership, Action and Change through Training

Partington J, Mayell C and Heap A, 1996, 'Results of the 1996 annual employment survey', *Labour Market Trends*, 105, 11, November, 461-467

Patel K, 1997, 'Tuition fee muddle hits Access courses', *Times Higher*, 12 September

Perman S, 1998, 'The learning age', *Adults Learning*, April, 26-27

Perri6 and Lawson G, 1997, 'A raw new deal', *'i' Magazine*, November, 14-15

Plummer G, 1998, 'Forget gender, class is still the real divide', *Times Educational Supplement* Research Focus, 23 January, 21

Power S, Whitty G, Edwards T and Wigfall V, 1998, 'Schoolboys and schoolwork: gender identification and academic achievement', *International Journal of Inclusive Education* 2/2, March-April, 135-153

Prestage M, 1998, 'Study deal on wheels', *Times Educational Supplement*, 20 March

Pringle K, 1996, 'Challenging oppressions, reconstructing masculinities', in Lloyd T and Wood T (eds) 1996, cited above

Pyke N, 1996, 'Male brain rattled by curriculum oestrogen', *Times Educational Supplement*, 15 March, 8

Qualifications and Curriculum Authority (QCA), 1998, *Can do better: raising boys' achievement in English*, London, Qualifications and Curriculum Authority

Rafferty F and Lewpkowska D, 1998, 'Boys should sit next to girls', *Times Educational Supplement*, 9 January

Redwood F, 1998, 'Top marks to the lads', *The Daily Telegraph*, 14 January

Reisenberger A and Crowther R, 1998, *Further education: giving young people a new start*, London, Further Education Development Agency

Riddell S, 1992, 'Gender and education: progressive and conservative forces in the balance' in Brown S and Riddell S (eds), *Class, race and gender in schools: a new agenda for policy and practice in Scottish education*, SCRE, minipaper 12, 44-53

Robertson D, 'Growth without equity? Reflections on the consequences for social cohesion of faltering progress on access to higher education', *Journal of Access Studies*, 12, Spring, 9-31

Rolfe H, Bryson A, and Metcalf H, 1996, *The effectiveness of TECs in achieving jobs and qualifications for disadvantaged groups*, HMSO

Rubenson K, 1998, *Adults readiness to learn: questioning lifelong learning for all.* Proceedings of the 39th US annual adult education research conference in San Antonio, May 15-16, Texas, A&M University, EHRD Department, College of Education, 257-262

Russell B, 1997, 'European cash helps lure jobless into college', *Times Educational Supplement*, 22 August

Ruxton S, 1996, 'Boys won't be boys: tackling the roots of male delinquency in Lloyd T and Wood T (eds), 1996, cited above, 77-92

Sargant N, 1993, *Learning for a purpose: participation in education and training by adults from ethnic minority communities*, Leicester, NIACE

Sargant N with Field J, Francis H, Schuller T, Tuckett, A, 1997, *The learning divide*, Leicester, NIACE

Sears N, 1998, 'Boys need action to help them read', *Times Educational Supplement*, 6 February, 10

Secretary of State for Education and Employment, 1998, *The learning age: a renaissance for a new Britain*, London, the Stationery Office

Segal L, 1989, *Is the future female?*, London, Virago

Seidler V, 1996, *Schooling from a masculinities perspective* in Lloyd T and Wood T (eds), *op cit*, 113-126

Sheriffe G, 1997, *Mentoring for African Caribbean men: action research report*, draft 1, City College Manchester

Shire D, 1997, 'Real level of black unemployment is double the official figure', *Working Brief*, May, 5-6

Sly F, Price A and Risdon A, 1997, 'Trends in labour market participation of ethnic groups, 1984-1996', *Labour Market Trends*, August

Social and Community Planning Research (SCPR), 1997, 1997 *National adult learning survey*, Social and Community Planning Research

Spencer D, 1997, 'Juvenile offenders gain inside knowledge', *Times Educational Supplement*, 29 August

Steedman H, 1998, 'A simple step that can bridge skills', *Times Educational Supplement*, 3 March

Stepney R, 1996, 'Being male means being mortal', *Independent*: section two, 8 January

Tett L, 1994, 'Where have all the men gone? Adult participation in community education', *Scottish Journal of ACE*, 1, 2, winter, 44-48

Tillsey C, 1995, 'Older workers: findings from the 1994 Labour Force Survey', *Employment Gazette*, April, 133-140

Tizzard B, Blatchford P, Burke J, Harguahar C and Plevis J, 1998, *Young children at school in the inner city*, Lawrence Erbaum Associates, London

Training Tomorrow, 1997, 'Homeless struggle for work', 11, 6, September

Travis A, 1998, 'Work scheme to include young prisoners', *The Guardian*, 4 February, 8

Trinder C and Worsley R, 1996, 'The labour market and older people – an update in Carnegie UK Trust, *The third age: the continuing challenge*, Dunfermline, 46-57

Tuckett A, 1997, 'There's no slick way to turn a tanker round', *Times Educational Supplement*, September, 32

Tyler C, 1997, 'Winging out of welfare', *Weekend*, 19-20 July

Tyesome T, 1998, 'Sex rules attitudes to school', *The Times Higher*, 8 May

Uden T, 1997, *Widening participation: routes to a learning society. A policy discussion paper*, Leicester, NIACE

Utley A, 1998, 'Parents alarmed at suicide risk', *The Times Higher*, 1 May

Walker D, 1996, 'In the shadow of big sister', *The Times Higher*, 23 August

Wallace W, 1998, 'Mullet over', *Times Educational Supplement*, 27 March

Webster D, 1997a, 'Promoting jobs could reduce lone parenthood', *Working Brief*, October, 20-22

Webster D, 1997b, 'Welfare to Work: why the theories behind the policies don't work', *Working Brief*, June, 10-11

Wells, A, 1997, 'Let's not neglect, the neglected', *Basic Skills*, June/July, 2-3

White M, 1990, 'Motivating education and training', *Policy Studies*, 10, 1, 29-40

Williams E, 1996, 'Despair beneath the macho surface', *Times Educational Supplement*, 15 March

Williams E, 1997a, 'Dropping a ladder into the pits of despair', *Times Educational Supplement*, 17 October

Williams E, 1997b, 'Excuse me, your future is waiting in the foyer', *Times Educational Supplement*, 11 July

Willis P, 1976, *Learning to labour: how working class kids get working class jobs*, Gower Press

Woltring L, 1996, 'Aiming for a new balance' in Lloyd T and Wood T (eds), 1996, *op cit*, 169-180

WRN, 1997, *Return*, September, London, Women Returners' Network

Woolford H and McDougall S, 1998, *The teacher as role model: the effects of teacher gender on boys' and girls' reading attainment*, Swansea, University of Wales

Young K, 1996, 'Why do men want to be victims?' in Lloyd T and Wood T (eds), *op cit*, 211-218

Young S, 1997, 'Job prospects worse for men than for women', *Times Educational Supplement*, 28 February, 15